TABLE OF CONTENTS

APPRECIATION

I am forever indebted to many teachers whose diligence in the Word has stimulated my thinking, stirred in me a holy reverence for God's Word, and contributed meaningfully to the realisation of this book.

This is written to all those who are appreciative of the glorious work of our Redeemer, in whom we have utterance and knowledge.

My wife, Olatee, has put up with the countless hours I used to put the thoughts in this book into written form. I took your feedback to heart Olatee. I love doing life with you

1

THE GIFT OF THE SPIRIT

35 And the angel answered and said unto her, The Holy Ghost shall come upon thee, and the power of the Highest shall overshadow thee: therefore also that holy thing which shall be born of thee shall be called the Son of God.
Luke 1: 35

What Gabriel said can be rendered as "The Holy Ghost shall come upon thee, even the power of the Highest." Notice that Gabriel is not telling Mary about two different things; one being "the Holy Spirit upon" and the other being "the power of the Highest". Instead, Gabriel used the term "the power of the Highest" to give a better explanation of the term "Holy Spirit upon". So, the "Holy Spirit upon" describes the operation of the power of the Highest. It describes the operation of God, the invisible but awesomely powerful one.

God is sometimes referred to as "the Holy" (see Psalms 78:41). The bible also states that God is a Spirit (see John 4:24). Therefore, it is easy to understand why He is referred to as the Holy Spirit. The Greek word that is translated "Ghost" is normally translated as spirit. Therefore, instead of Holy Ghost we could say Holy Spirit.

Capitals matter

The observant bible reader knows that it does not matter whether most words in the Bible start with capitals or not. Therefore, there is no meaningful difference between Tongues and tongues or between Salvation and salvation. However, it matters a great deal when certain words begin with capitals or not. There is implied meaning in capitalisation of these words. For that reason, God is not the same as god. God refers to the Father while god has a variety of meanings some of which describes false deities. You can appreciate the confusion that follows from disregarding the capitalisation of these particular class of words.

The New Testament was written in Greek. In the early Greek manuscripts, all the letters were either all lower case or all capitalised with no spaces in between the words (known as scriptio continua). If we were to use the text of the KJV, John 3:6 would originally have been written this way:

THATWHICHISBORNOFTHEFLESHISFLESHANDTHAT WHICHISBORNOFTHESPIRITISSPIRIT
John 3: 6

That is hard to read.

It is easier to read the same text if it is spaced this way:

THAT WHICH IS BORN OF THE FLESH IS FLESH AND THAT WHICH IS BORN OF THE SPIRIT IS SPIRIT
John 3: 6

It is easier to catch the meaning of the text if it is spaced and capitalised this way:

That which is born of the flesh is flesh; and that which is born of the Spirit is spirit.
John 3: 6

It is the same Greek word that has been translated as Spirit and spirit. Yet, the meaning is clear when we capitalise one and keep the other all lower case. Capitals matter. Spirit doesn't mean the same as spirit. Spirit is reserved for God the Giver of life, while spirit is used for that which is born of the Spirit. The term "spirit" has a variety of meanings in all languages. In English, spirit could refer to alcoholic drinks, intention, slant, God or even demons. Given the varied range of meanings, we should use the context of the scriptural text to reveal what spirit means in a given instance rather than attaching fixed meaning to the word "spirit". When we give fixed meanings to words without considering context, the result is confusion.

God means what He has said in His Word and He wants us to know the meaning of the words He has used to convey His Word. It matters whether God says Spirit or spirit. Although, spirit has various meanings, in this book, we'll limit our conversation to God as Spirit and man as spirit.

17 Now the Lord is that Spirit: and where the Spirit of the Lord is, there is liberty.
2 Corinthians 3: 17

In this instance, Spirit refers to the person of the Lord Jesus. The Lord who is that Spirit is the Lord Jesus Christ.

7 He that hath an ear, let him hear what the Spirit saith unto the churches; To him that overcometh will I give to eat of the tree of life, which is in the midst of the paradise of God.
Revelation 2: 7

Notice that the Spirit speaking in the book of Revelation is the Lord Jesus.

25 And when they agreed not among themselves, they departed, after that Paul had spoken one word, Well spake the Holy Ghost by Esaias the prophet unto our fathers,
Acts 28: 25

The Holy Ghost that spoke to the Jews via the ministry of the Prophets refers to God.

3 But Peter said, Ananias, why hath Satan filled thine heart to lie to the Holy Ghost, and to keep back part of the price of the land?
Acts 5: 3

Rather than say that Ananias had lied to God, Peter said the same thing by saying that Ananias had lied to the Holy Ghost. Peter refers to God as the Holy Ghost.

It is the same word that is used for man as spirit and God as Spirit. Therefore, in many other instances in the New Testament scriptures, it is notoriously difficult at first glance, to tell whether spirit should be "Spirit", which refers to God the Giver or "spirit", which often refers to His divine nature that we partake of as His gift to us in Christ. We can only tell by paying attention to details.

I believe that it would have made more sense had the translators just left the Greek word in these verses where spirit is mentioned. Instead, with the best of intentions, these translators have not just translated but interpreted for they already determined for us where it is Spirit and not spirit. If all we do is follow the Bible translators in this regard, there is a lot of confusion that lingers on in the mind of the honest student of the Word.

16 The Spirit itself beareth witness with our spirit, that we are the children of God
Romans 8: 16

In the Greek, the case used for the two spirits in this verse is the same. The writers in the Greek did not differentiate. The translators should capitalise the S in Spirit when the subject matter is God. However, they often used Spirit when they should have used spirit. We use the context to know whether the spirit refers to God or not.

Here, the Spirit who bears witness refers to God, who is the Giver. The spirit that receives the joint witness refers to the nature of God born within His children – this is His gift to us. All that have this spirit as God's gift are the children of God. The spirit that we received from God is as holy as God is holy. More importantly, the Giver is the Spirit and the gift given by the Giver is spirit. Although both are the same Greek word, the two spirits do not refer to the same person.

Various terms for the spirit

I have always felt that Romans 8 should be called the chapter of the spirit for it is filled with various terms for the spirit. We find in it such terms as "spirit of Christ", "spirit of him" and "spirit of God".

It has been pointed out that the first time Paul clearly speaks of God, the Holy Ghost, in this chapter is when he speaks of the Spirit that bears witness with our spirit. The spirit that bears witness with our spirit is the Holy Ghost. Prior to this, the various usages of spirit described in Romans 8 are all descriptions of the born again human spirit which is God's gift to man in Christ. Even Paul's reference to the spirit by which we are led refers to the fact that God has given man His spirit as a gift to lead man out of spiritual death into the status of sons (see Romans 8:14). As sinners, we were "in the flesh". As saints, we are "in the spirit" (see Romans 8:9). We were led out of "in the flesh" to "in the spirit" by receiving the spirit as God's gift in Christ. This is salvation.

8 He therefore that despiseth, despiseth not man, but God, who hath also given unto us his holy Spirit.
1 Thessalonians 4: 8

Paul wants these Thessalonians to know that God has already given His holy spirit. All that God gave, He gave in Christ. As the Giver, God has given us the singular gift - His holy spirit.

Except we pay attention, the biases of traditional reading will cause us to see the Giver, the Holy Spirit, in many places where we should have seen the gift, the holy spirit. If we see the Giver where we should have seen His gift to us in Christ, we allow the thief rob us of the riches of understanding contained in the Word. We do this easily.

Not only has God given His gift, we are recipients of the same. Consider this:

38 Then Peter said unto them, Repent, and be baptized every one of you in the name of Jesus Christ for the remission of sins, and ye shall receive the gift of the Holy Ghost.
Acts 2: 38

What did Peter mean by "ye shall receive the gift of the Holy Ghost" as he preached on the day of Pentecost?

Peter had shown that God had fulfilled David's prophecy by raising Christ from the dead (see Acts 2:32). As a result, God had made Jesus both Lord and Christ (see Acts 2:36). The Gospel within Peter's sermon had given that crowd all the ingredients that Romans 10:9 demands for salvation – salvation is received by believing in your heart that God has raised Jesus from the dead and confessing Him as Lord. So, Peter was discussing the New Birth.

We also know that Peter was discussing salvation because the consequence of Peter's preaching was, "the Lord added to the church daily such as should be saved" (see Acts 2: 47). Therefore, Peter was offering salvation to the crowd.

The careful student will note that while Romans 10 said nothing about water baptism, Peter preached it on the day of Pentecost. This was because Peter did not yet know the truth about salvation in the New Testament not requiring water baptism. When he preached about the resurrection of Jesus from the dead and His Lordship, he had provided his audience with all that they needed for the baptism. The spirit baptism, which happens within those that believe the Gospel today is the true fulfilment of the water baptism of previous ages. This was still very early in the history of the Church and the truths of the Church were still secrets that were not yet plainly taught in the Church (see Romans 16:2-26 & Ephesians 3:4-5). The Lord Jesus would later use the writings of Paul to reveal that this period is the dispensation of God's grace (see Ephesians 3:2).

The text is better translated as "ye shall receive the gift of Holy Spirit" because the Greek has no "the" in "the Holy Ghost" and Ghost is the Greek word translated as spirit elsewhere. The Greek words translated gift here is 'dorea', which describes the manner in which this gift is given – with no strings attached. This means that it is freely given. Peter's assertion on the day of Pentecost, "ye shall receive the gift of Holy Spirit" is referring to the salvation of the human spirit. Therefore, this text should read, "ye shall receive the gift of holy spirit." Peter was letting the people know that the gift that was poured out on the day of Pentecost was the gift of holy spirit. It was this holy spirit that the disciples had received from God. It is this same spirit that was now available to be received through believing Peter's sermon.

The promise of the Father

We can better appreciate Peter's sermon when we understand that the Lord Jesus had taught the disciples extensively about the holy spirit as the promise of the Father before He ascended to heaven.

4 And, being assembled together with them, commanded them that they should
not depart from Jerusalem, but wait for the promise of the Father, which, saith
he, ye have heard of me. 5 For John truly baptized with water; but ye shall be
baptized with the Holy Ghost not many days hence.

Acts 1: 4 - 5

Notice that Jesus had taught His disciples about waiting for a specific promise that He referred to as the promise of the Father.

Waiting for the promise is an interesting play on words. These disciples couldn't be waiting for God to give the promise since God had already made that promise through what He told Abraham when He preached the Gospel to him long before the disciples were born (see Galatians 3:8). These disciples were waiting for what had been promised. In other words the fulfilment of the promise. There was something greater on the way. He referred to this as being "baptized with the Holy Ghost". These disciples already knew water baptism through John the Baptist. In fact, John had prophesied that just as water was his medium of baptism, Jesus would prove His greater work by making the spirit the medium of His own baptism (see Luke 3:16). So, Jesus wasn't promising them another water baptism but the fulfilment of the water baptism in the one baptism of the spirit (see Ephesians 4:5).

Jesus had taught them that the Holy Spirit is the promise of the Father. This Holy Spirit is the gift given by the Father who is the Giver. Therefore, the gift of holy spirit is God's nature in His saints. It is the recreated spirit of men.

On the day of Pentecost, the disciples were filled with the holy spirit in the capacity of sons. They became brand new creations. This was the fulfilment of Jesus' prophecy that they would be baptized with the holy ghost "not many days hence".

Luke captures this fact that Jesus taught about the specific promise:

49 And, behold, I send the promise of my Father upon you: but tarry ye in the city of Jerusalem, until ye be endued with power from on high.
Luke 24: 49

The Lord Jesus specifically told His disciples to wait in Jerusalem for the promise of His Father. This promise is being clothed with power from on high. This is the same thing as being born again or being born from above.

Being clothed with power from on high and being born from above both refer to the baptism with the holy spirit. This helps us see that the holy spirit that we receive at the New Birth is the power of God in us and it is the power from on high.

The Lord Jesus is the Giver today

33 Therefore being by the right hand of God exalted, and having received of the Father the promise of the Holy Ghost, he hath shed forth this, which ye now see and hear.

Acts 2: 33

God's promise was the Holy Ghost. This is the gift given, so it refers to the holy ghost.

In order to appreciate this piece of scripture, there are two key events that we are to remember – the resurrection of the Son of God and His seating. At His resurrection, the Lord Jesus received a new kind of life. The Lord Jesus then used the forty days after His resurrection to teach His disciples about the great event that was on the way – the great event was His seating, which would lead to the giving of the promise. The giving of the gift was so important that after His resurrection Jesus prepared His disciples for the giving of the promise in Luke 24 and Acts 1. At His glorification and exaltation at the Father's right hand, He received the promise of the ages, the gift of the holy spirit for a new type of humanity.

When God exalted Christ Jesus as the head of the Church, God who used to be the Giver of the spirit, gave the Lord Jesus, once and for all time, the promised spirit as gift. Thus, the Lord Jesus is the Giver of the spirit today. The Lord Jesus, through His exaltation as the seated One, has radically altered our pneumatology (pneuma is from the Greek word for spirit. I use pneumatology to mean the study of the Word's use of the term "spirit"). Our pneumatology is to be an offshoot of our Christology. There is a big difference between the giving of the spirit in the Old Testament and giving it subsequent to the glorification of the Lord Jesus. Since after His seating at God's right hand, God is no longer the Giver of the spirit as gift, the Lord Jesus is. The Lord gives the holy spirit as earnest and seal within the saint in a permanent way because of His accomplishments as the Redeemer (see Ephesians 1:13). Notice this fact: The Lord Jesus shed forth what could be heard at Pentecost. Thus, the Lord Jesus as the life-giving Spirit generated the language of tongues and the saint receives this through the gift of holy spirit within the saint. The saint then speaks the tongues out. Therefore, speaking in tongues is hearing the risen Lord and voicing what you hear Him say by faith. This is a key way that the saint knows and understand the things that God has freely given. It is how we commune with God spirit-to-Spirit, (see 1 Corinthians 2:12).

The Old Testament teaches salvation through faith

The truth concerning the promise of the spirit in The New testament is verifiable in the Old Testament. We rob ourselves of seeing it by neglecting the Old Testament scriptures. Paul gave a powerful charge to Timothy that challenges our slant towards all scripture and sets the proper tone of true bible study.

14 But continue thou in the things which thou hast learned and hast been assured of, knowing of whom thou hast learned them; 15 And that from a child thou hast known the holy scriptures, which are able to make thee wise unto salvation through faith which is in Christ Jesus. 16 All scripture is given by inspiration of God, and is profitable for doctrine, for reproof, for correction, for instruction in righteousness:
2 Timothy 3: 14 - 16

The holy scriptures that Timothy had known from a little child are the Jewish Old Testament. Timothy is perhaps Paul's foremost disciple to whom he had personally taught the mystery as well as other truths of the New Testament. Yet, he discloses to Timothy the futility of attempting to gain mastery of the Gospel without continuing to read all of the Old Testament. He assures Timothy that when considered fully, it is the reading of all of the Old Testament that is able to make him wise unto salvation through faith which is in Christ Jesus! All of the Old Testament properly read furnishes us with a well-grounded revelation of Jesus. Paul wanted Timothy to see that Jesus is the logic and true content of the Jewish Old Testament. Without studying the Old Testament, there is no way that anyone can become wise or understand faith in Christ clearly. Therefore, it is unwise and contrary to the New Testament to abandon the study of the Old Testament.

We mustn't study the Old Testament only because we recognise that it is inspired. We should really study it in order that we might grasp faith in Christ thoroughly.

The chief purpose of all of scripture is that it supplies reproof. Reproof means to supply evidence or conviction. This is particularly helpful since the things of the spirit are experiential, and one person's experience will differ slightly from that of another. Therefore, we cannot make our experience the foundation of our pneumatology. Our pneumatology must be grounded in scripture and not merely experience. God has designed His Word as the strongest means for supplying this evidence to His saints. The Lord has given us abundance of evidence concerning the things of the holy spirit through the Word.

8 And the scripture, foreseeing that God would justify the heathen through faith, preached before the gospel unto Abraham, saying, In thee shall all nations be blessed.
Galatians 3: 8

At the heart of the Gospel that He preached to Abraham is God's promise to bless all men. This blessing is something that only God can bring to pass.

14 That the blessing of Abraham might come on the Gentiles through Jesus Christ; that we might receive the promise of the Spirit through faith.
Galatians 3: 14

The blessing of Abraham could only come on the Gentiles through Jesus Christ.

What is the blessing of Abraham? The blessing that God proclaimed to Abraham was the giving of the holy spirit through faith in Christ, whom God would raise from the dead. The reception of the promised spirit is Abraham's blessing. The spirit as gift is the promise contained within the Gospel. Faith in Christ is receiving the spirit on the basis of what Christ has done. The reception of the spirit as gift recreates man. It is the status of holiness and power.

In different ages, various terms were employed throughout the Bible in describing God's promise of the spirit, which is the blessing.

For example, in Jesus' conversation with Nicodemus:

4 Nicodemus saith unto him, How can a man be born when he is old? can he
enter the second time into his mother's womb, and be born? 5 Jesus answered,
Verily, verily, I say unto thee, Except a man be born of water and of the Spirit,
he cannot enter into the kingdom of God. 6 That which is born of the flesh is
flesh; and that which is born of the Spirit is spirit. 7 Marvel not that I said
unto thee, Ye must be born again.
8 The wind bloweth where it listeth, and thou hearest the sound thereof, but canst
not tell whence it cometh, and whither it goeth: so is every one that is born of the
Spirit. 9 Nicodemus answered and said unto him, How can these things be? 10
Jesus answered and said unto him, Art thou a master of Israel, and knowest
not these things?
John 3:4 - 10

The term translated "again" in "born again" means "from above". Jesus's told Nicodemus that man needed to be born from above. He explained this truth to Nicodemus by saying, "Except a man be born of water and of the Spirit, he cannot enter into the kingdom of God."

Before we fix western meanings to what Jesus told Nicodemus about being born of water, we must remember that Jesus had said to Nicodemus, "Art thou a master of Israel, and knowest not these things?" This would mean that Jesus knew that when He spoke of man needing to be born of water and of the spirit, He was not saying anything new to Nicodemus that was not already contained within the holy scriptures. Whatever being born of water and of the Spirit means, the gist of it is captured within the Old Testament scriptures.

This is most readily seen in Ezekiel's prophecy about what God said that He would do with water and spirit.

25 Then will I sprinkle clean water upon you, and ye shall be clean: from all

your filthiness, and from all your idols, will I cleanse you. 26 A new heart also will I give you, and a new spirit will I put within you: and I will take away the stony heart out of your flesh, and I will give you an heart of flesh.
Ezekiel 36:25 - 26

God promised, "I will cleanse you." He would cleanse man from filthiness by sprinkling clean water upon man. This is a parable. The water is not literal but spiritual.

This cleansing is explained by God giving man a new heart by personally putting a new spirit within him or her. God cleanses man by giving him a new spirit. Ezekiel's prophecy shows a water and spirit connection.

The spirit is the water

There are several instances in scriptures where spirit and water are used as equivalent terms (see John 4:13-14, Isaiah 43:3 & John 3:5). John's inspired commentary on the spirit and water connection is most illuminating.

38 He that believeth on me, as the scripture hath said, out of his belly shall flow rivers of living water. 39 (But this spake he of the Spirit, which they that believe on him should receive: for the Holy Ghost was not yet given; because that Jesus was not yet glorified.)
John 7:38 - 39

It is most unusual to find in scripture a commentary on something Jesus said. When Jesus spoke about the rivers of living water He was speaking about the Holy Ghost that was not yet given. Since this Holy Ghost is given, we know this is a gift and not a reference to the Giver; therefore, this should be holy ghost and not "Holy Ghost".

When Jesus spoke of the living water flowing out of Him towards those that believe, He was showing that men would believe on Him and He would give them the living water, even the gift of holy spirit.

The holy spirit that men receive as a result of believing on Jesus is that promise, which is the gift of a new spirit in man. Therefore, Jesus is prophesying that He would be the Giver of the gift of holy ghost, which we receive from the Lord Jesus by faith. At His glorification, the Lord Jesus created one new man. He creates something new inside each person that believes in Him. This new man is the new nature He gives to all saints (see Ephesians 4:24, Galatians 6:15 & 2 Corinthians 5:17). The Lord Jesus, by His resurrection, created a new order, even a new species of men called saints. He is the creator of the Church and without His creative activity, the Church would not exist.

When Ezekiel speaks of water, we are to understand that Ezekiel was not describing literal water; therefore, we shouldn't go looking for flowing streams or stagnant ponds. Ezekiel was speaking of spiritual water. It was not until after His exaltation by the Father that Jesus baptised anyone for the first time. While on earth, He did not baptise anyone (see John 4:2). When Jesus finally baptised men, He baptised with spiritual water, which is His great gift of holy spirit.

Although our English bibles say "the Holy Ghost was not yet given", this text doesn't have the word "given". Therefore, it should read, "the holy ghost was not yet". In other words, the holy spirit that would be received as a result of the glorification of Christ would be so totally different from what men had known up till that time that it is as good as that which had never been. Even if we keep the word "given", we still know that the holy spirit of which Jesus speaks will be massively different because John is emphatic that it was not yet given!

Thus, the gift of the holy spirit that the saints have today is radically different from what the saints had prior to the ascension and seating of Christ at the Father's right hand. On this side of the cross, we have the spirit without measure whereas they did not. The gift of holy spirit brings about spiritual development in the saint, whereas that wasn't the case prior to Jesus' death. Prior to Jesus' seating, one does not have the spirit just because one is a saint. Only a few saints had the spirit and they had the spirit upon. Today, all who believe receive the promise of the spirit as God's free gift in Christ. This spirit has been sealed into the nature of every born again one. The spirit is upon because it is first within the saint. The holy spirit is the identity of the saint today. These differences are ours in Christ glorified. The saint can confidently say that the gift of holy spirit that every saint has today never existed prior to the glorification of the Lord Jesus in His exaltation by God. No one prior to Jesus ever had this new creation.

Paul gives us some insight into how God executed His marvellous plan of cleansing man by supplying him with the water, which is the gift of holy spirit.

5 And hope maketh not ashamed; because the love of God is shed abroad in our hearts by the Holy Ghost which is given unto us. 6 For when we were yet without strength, in due time Christ died for the ungodly.
Romans 5:5 - 6

We know that the greatest display and revelation of God's love is in the person of Jesus. The Love of God is in Christ Jesus (see Romans 8:39).

That term "the Holy Ghost which is given unto us" is God's gift of His promise – the holy spirit. The new spirit is the strength that God gave to the ungodly. No saint lacks power for there cannot be saint without the gift of spirit.

God did not pour His love into our hearts by giving us day and night or houses and cars. It is explained specifically as Christ dying on the cross for the ungodly – Christ is God's love to us. God's love is in the past and enters our hearts as we see the finished works of Christ. The work of God's spirit in our heart is to bring us in contact with the truth of God's love. We let that love into our hearts as we believe what God was displaying through the giving of the holy spirit to us in Christ Jesus.

The New Birth, which is the receiving of the gift of holy spirit in Christ, is God fulfilling what He said through Ezekiel about putting a new spirit within man. Ezekiel also spoke about sprinkling clean water, which will cleanse man completely. The summary of Ezekiel's prophecy is that the spirit is the cleansing water.

Jesus expected Nicodemus to grasp the spirit-water connection.

Paul continued expanding on this thought of baptism and circumcision.

11 In whom also ye are circumcised with the circumcision made without hands, in putting off the body of the sins of the flesh by the circumcision of Christ: 12 Buried with him in baptism, wherein also ye are risen with him through the faith of the operation of God, who hath raised him from the dead.
Colossians 2:11 - 12

Christ did not physically circumcise the saint. The circumcision of Christ is the cutting off of the old man. The destruction of spiritual death. Just as the circumcision is not literal, so also the baptism is not literal but spiritual. This baptism, which is the circumcision made without human hands isn't something that one man did to another. God has sprinkled clean water upon us in that we have been buried with Christ in baptism and raised together with Christ. God did this in Christ in raising us together with Christ in His resurrection. We did not cleanse or raise ourselves nor did we baptise ourselves. The prophesied baptism is an act that God has levied upon Himself to perform and He fulfilled this when He baptised us.

Speaking of the gift of holy spirit, consider this text:

13 In whom ye also trusted, after that ye heard the word of truth, the gospel of your salvation: in whom also after that ye believed, ye were sealed with that holy Spirit of promise
Ephesians 1: 13

The Holy Spirit here is the gift given and not the Giver; therefore, it refers to the human spirit. Our Father God wants us to know that after we believed and received the Gospel, we were immediately sealed with that holy spirit of promise. The promise of God which we received through believing the Gospel is the holy spirit as seal.

The spirit as seal is the guarantee of a possession that can never be removed and confirms that the saint belongs to God forever. This holy spirit is God's nature, which is His gift that He seals into the spirit of the saint. This holy spirit is how God secures us and guarantees everything associated with godliness.

Paul repeated this truth of the spirit as seal to the Corinthians when he said, "Who hath also sealed us, and given the earnest of the Spirit in our hearts" (see 2 Corinthians 1: 22).

Paul did not teach the Corinthians one seal and the Ephesians another. Notice that the earnest of the spirit is in our hearts. It is the same spirit that is seal that is also an earnest. Earnest is a form of guarantee or deposit that assures the one in possession of the deposit of more to come. The seal of God in the life of a saint today is the recreated human spirit. This is how you know you are of God – His gift to us is His divine nature which He gave by giving us the spirit. Therefore, this divine nature in man is the holy spirit. We are partakers of His divine nature (see 2 Peter 1:4).

2

THE SPIRIT OF TRUTH

33. And with many such parables spake he the word unto them, as they were able to hear it. 34. But without a parable spake he not unto them: and when they were alone, he expounded all things to his disciples.
Mark 4: 33 - 34

In His earthly ministry, the Lord Jesus taught a lot using parables.

41. Then Peter said unto him, Lord, speakest thou this parable unto us, or even to all?
Luke 12: 41

The Word is not silent on the fact that the disciples could not tell who the audience of Jesus' parable was.

6. This parable spake Jesus unto them: but they understood not what things they were which he spake unto them.
John 10: 6

At other times, the disciples heard Jesus' parable but did not understand them.

25. These things have I spoken unto you in proverbs: but the time cometh, when I shall no more speak unto you in proverbs, but I shall shew you plainly of the

Father.
John 16: 25

The Lord acknowledged that in John 14-16, He had taught them in parables but He looked forward to a day when He would not more be forced to speak to them in parables. He was teaching them about the Father but He could only say it in parables. Those three chapters contain a continuous flow of thoughts that Jesus wanted to communicate plainly.

29. His disciples said unto him, Lo, now speakest thou plainly, and speakest no proverb.
John 16: 29

As the disciples continued to listen to Jesus, they finally said, "Now you speak plainly." Jesus was speaking of salvation. His disciples believed He was a prophet but they did not yet understand or believe the Gospel message that God would raise Jesus from the dead (see Luke 24:19-25).

20. At that day ye shall know that I am in my Father, and ye in me, and I in you.
John 14: 20

Jesus spoke of the day in which we will know that He is in us as we are in Him and He is in the Father. This is the language of identification, which is amplified in the Epistles. Jesus is prophesying that will know the reality of the fulfilment of union with our Father God.

He that hath my commandments, and keepeth them, he it is that loveth me: and he that loveth me shall be loved of my Father, and I will love him, and will manifest myself to him.
John 14: 21

The reason for Jesus' parables in the book of John was to reveal to His hearers the love that will cause Him to manifest Himself to those that keep His commandments.

The Gospel contrasted with the Epistles

Why did John write this record?

31. But these are written, that ye might believe that Jesus is the Christ, the Son of God; and that believing ye might have life through his name.
John 20: 31

The Gospel of John was written to get the non-believer to believe.

13. These things have I written unto you that believe on the name of the Son of God; that ye may know that ye have eternal life, and that ye may believe on the name of the Son of God.
1 John 5: 13

The Epistles are written to those who have already believed. The intent of the Epistles is to help the believer come into knowledge. Knowledge is awareness of that which has been accomplished. The Epistles show that the saints don't need more faith but an understanding of those things already believed. The Epistles build faith by giving us the knowledge of what we already believed. In the Gospel of John, we believed that Jesus would manifest Himself to us. In the Epistle, we are to know that this has been fulfilled.

3. How that by revelation he made known unto me the mystery; (as I wrote afore in few words, 4. Whereby, when ye read, ye may understand my knowledge in the mystery of Christ)
Ephesians 3: 3 - 4

Paul has written so that the saints that read his knowledge might have understanding of the mystery by it. The Epistles give a clear explanation of the mystery. The mystery refers to the dark sayings and parables prior to the resurrection of Jesus. We use the Epistles to explain all the scriptures that came before the resurrection of Jesus. Although, the New Testament operates by the law of faith, Paul does not write in order that saints might believe. The saint is to grow up by understanding the truth that was initially believed. For the saint in Christ, the law of faith is more of understanding and knowledge than of believing. As people of faith, we are to have a solid grasp of what we believed in the Gospel. We press on from believing to knowing.

Again, a new commandment I write unto you, which thing is true in him and in you: because the darkness is past, and the true light now shineth.
1 John 2: 8

The light that shines is the thing that is true in Christ and in us. Our proof that the thing that is true in Christ has been made true in the saint is this light that shines. The light that shines is the recreated spirit. This true light that shines is the light associated with the truth of the new commandment. The new commandment is not another set of words etched on stones, rather it is the documentation of the life of God in man. In the Gospels, John calls this the spirit of truth. The spirit of truth is the spirit of the reality of what Jesus has done. All that Jesus has accomplished is only experienced through this spirit. The possession of the spirit is the proof that what Christ is, we are. The Epistles teach the saints about the things that are already true in Christ and in the saint. The fact is that the darkness of spiritual death can never reign over the saint. The recreated spirit is the anointing that we received of Christ. That spirit is the proof or truth.

We are the house of God

4. For every house is builded by some man; but he that built all things is God. 5. And Moses verily was faithful in all his house, as a servant, for a testimony of those things which were to be spoken after; 6. But Christ as a son over his own house; whose house are we, if we hold fast the confidence and the rejoicing of the hope firm unto the end.
Hebrews 3: 4-6

The truth is that God is the one that builds all things. Why then did Moses build the tabernacle in the wilderness? Moses built the tabernacle in the wilderness as a testimony to unbelieving Israel of the things that were to be spoken afterwards. These things were spoken afterwards by Jesus. What Moses physically demonstrated to the unbelieving and Jesus testified of by His teaching, we have the reality in our spirits. God has built us.

We are the father's household on account of faith in Christ.

2. In my Father's house are many mansions: if it were not so, I would have told you. I go to prepare a place for you.
John 14: 2

When Jesus said that the father's household has many mansions, Jesus was speaking to those who are to believe in God by believing in Jesus. In particular, His disciples believed in God by believing that Jesus stood in the prophet's office. However, they did not yet believe in Jesus as the Saviour. So, Jesus said, "believe also in me." The Lord Jesus was trying to convey the truths about God as Father but He couldn't say it plainly. This is parabolic language. The mansions refer to the saint as the house that God built. In plain speech, each saint is a mansion in the household. Jesus was confirming that He would be going to prepare us as the Father's house.

3. And if I go and prepare a place for you, I will come again, and receive you unto myself; that where I am, there ye may be also.
John 14: 3

Jesus was emphatic - I will come again.

Jesus definitely said, "I will not leave you comfortless: I will come to you" (see John 14: 18).

23. Jesus answered and said unto him, if a man love me, he will keep my words: and my Father will love him, and we will come unto him, and make our abode with him.
John 14: 23

Jesus shows that the Father's love will cause the Father and the Lord to come to man and abide with man. The statements of Jesus can be summarised by the fact that He will come again when He prepares our place as sons in the Father's family.

16. And I will pray the Father, and he shall give you another Comforter, that he may abide with you for ever; 17. Even the Spirit of truth; whom the world cannot receive, because it seeth him not, neither knoweth him: but ye know him; for he dwelleth with you, and shall be in you.
John 14: 16-17

Jesus repeatedly said "I will come again." How did He come? He said it is by the Father's act of giving another comforter to man. The spirit that was with them was going to be in them.

Observe that in explaining His coming again, the Lord introduces another asides Himself and the Father. He calls this new entity the spirit of truth. The Lord has come as the spirit of truth. Truth is the fulfilment of that teaching, "I will come again." The things that Jesus said would be done are now done. The spirit of truth is the spirit as confirmation that He that said He would come again has come as another comforter. The spirit that He has given us is the truth confirmed in us forever.

The Lord Jesus has manifested Himself as the spirit within us. The Father and Son abide within us as the spirit of truth. It is by the indwelling of the spirit of truth that we have proof of our oneness with the Lord. It is by receiving the spirit that we know that we are in Christ as Christ is in us. Our reality is that the Father abides with us by the comforter abiding within. He is in us by the comforter, even the spirit sent within us. The Lord shows that the comforter is the holy spirit that the Father sends in His name. "In His name" means on the basis of the standing and works of the Son (see John 14:26).

29. And now I have told you before it come to pass, that, when it is come to pass, ye might believe.
John 14: 29

This is the statement of the promise. We know that the prophecy of Jesus has come to pass. It is now fact. The spirit of truth is the reality of that prophecy.

Praising God as He has praised us

Paul referred to this as spiritual blessings in Christ:

3. Blessed be the God and Father of our Lord Jesus Christ, who hath blessed us with all spiritual blessings in heavenly places in Christ:
Ephesians 1: 3

Paul encourages us to bless God because God has already blessed all saints with all spiritual blessings in Christ. Blessing God is the believer's response to God. We pick our response from His activity. The height of spirituality is ability to recognise God's movements in Christ and to magnify that above all else. God first speaks well of us and then in response we are to speak well of Him. Being in Christ is highest praise. Our status in Christ is God's handiwork. We see this handiwork and praise God because He has already praised us in Christ.

The word translated blessed in "Blessed be the God" is an adjective (eulogetos) derived from a verb (eulogeo) and eulogeo is itself derived from two words "eu" and logos". "Eu" means well done or good, while "logos" refers to the summation of thoughts, logic and ideas. Since God is the recipient of our "blessed", and we are the ones "blessing" God, logos describes our access into the full orb of God's thoughts and ideas, which is Christ. "Blessed be God" would mean we are saying those things that agree with God about His well-executed calculations for the saints in Christ. What we say about God is to be in line with His spectacular show in Christ.

It is not our feelings, emotions or experiences. We access His thoughts and these shapes what we say about Him. You could say that we praise God because He has given us His highest praise in Christ. Spiritual blessings refer to the unseen blessings, which would be blessing of the spirit. God has blessed us by giving us the spirit. In context, God has calculated that the way to secure His plan is to place all spiritual blessings in Christ. The spiritual things are those things that pertain to the unseen realm. Thus, God's plan is centered on the blessings of the spirit. Christ has put the riches of His grace in the spirit of man. The spirit is proof of possession of the blessings.

Paul then lists the blessings of the spirit as:

4. According as he hath chosen us in him before the foundation of the world, that we should be holy and without blame before him in love: 5. Having predestinated us unto the adoption of children by Jesus Christ to himself, according to the good pleasure of his will, 6. To the praise of the glory of his grace, wherein he hath made us accepted in the beloved. 7. In whom we have redemption through his blood, the forgiveness of sins, according to the riches of his grace; 8. Wherein he hath abounded toward us in all wisdom and prudence; 9. Having made known unto us the mystery of his will, according to his good pleasure which he hath purposed in himself: 10. That in the dispensation of the fulness of times he might gather together in one all things in Christ, both which are in heaven, and which are on earth; even in him: 11. In whom also we have obtained an inheritance, being predestinated according to the purpose of him who worketh all things after the counsel of his own will: 12. That we should be to the praise of his glory, who first trusted in Christ.
Ephesians 1: 4 - 12

All these are the blessings of the spirit or spiritual blessings.

How do we know that the marvellous listing of the blessings are so?

13. In whom ye also trusted, after that ye heard the word of truth, the gospel of your salvation: in whom also after that ye believed, ye were sealed with that holy Spirit of promise,
Ephesians 1: 13

God's proof to us that the blessings are ours is that He gave to us the holy spirit of promise. The terminology "spirit of promise" means that the spirit is the proof that the promise is fulfilled. If that spirit had not been given as gift, all that God ever said is found to be false. Since the spirit is God's proof, it means that God wants His performance to be measured by what we find within the gift of holy spirit. All the riches of God's grace in redemption are given to us in the holy spirit of promise. In other words, none of these blessings are located outside the spirit. The spirit as seal means that the spirit is the proof of ownership of all these blessings stated. We speak well of God by not looking any further than the spirit as the status of our inheritance in Christ.

This means that the gift of holy spirit that the Lord Jesus gave to man in the New Birth is the true measure of the credibility of God. All that God has promised is made real to us in the spirit of promise. The spirit is the status and proof of sonship, tongues, interpretation and prophecy.

God is justified in the spirit

Paul marvelled that God wants the spirit in man to be His credentials:

16. And without controversy great is the mystery of godliness: God was manifest in the flesh, justified in the Spirit, seen of angels, preached unto the Gentiles, believed on in the world, received up into glory.
1 Timothy 3: 16

The mystery of godliness is explained as God being manifest in the flesh in the man Jesus, for God was at work in Christ (see 2 Corinthians 5:18-19). The activities of Christ perfectly explain God. The Lord was raised again for our justification (see Romans 4: 25). So, "God was justified in the Spirit" refers to man's righteousness on the basis of the resurrection of Christ. Thus, the Church is the spirits of just men made perfect (see Hebrews 12: 23). God was justified in that He has given the spirit as righteousness to those that believe that He raised Jesus from the dead. It is by His gift of a recreated spirit that God was proved righteous or right. If that gift had not been given, all that God ever said is found to be false. God has hinged His reputation on His ability to provide a new spirit in men. This spirit, that God takes so much pride in and wants to be measured by, is not angelic. It is His gift of spirit in the Born Again man.

When Paul said, "seen of angels", he is saying that the angels saw God most clearly when they saw the spirit of just men made perfect. The angels see God most clearly when they see the spirit that God has put in those that believe. The spirit changed man and the change in man caused angels to see God in a clearer way. The message that the world is to believe through our preaching is that godliness is definable in terms of the new spirit that God puts in man. God is most glorified in that He has received man into the glory of sonship. He accomplished this by His activity in providing a new spirit in men by the resurrection of Jesus. Thus, the mystery of godliness is men transformed by receiving a new spirit.

The spirit with which each saint is sealed, is the gift of God. That spirit is not of this earth or of Adam. The spirit is born of God. It is the inheritance that Jesus as the life-giving Spirit gives to the believer and it is how man is received up into glory, which tells us that it is connected with the heavenlies. The body of the saint is of the dust of this earth and the means by which the saint interacts with the earth and the realm of the seen. This means that the New Birth is Christ introducing the heavenlies into the body of man so that the body becomes the temple of the spirit. Thus, each saint interacts simultaneously with heavenly things via the spirit and earthly things via the body. The saint is the embodiment of the heavenlies in a physical body. Thus, each saint is an enigma worthy of study. The mystery of godliness is so great, that Paul had to pray, in his letter to the saints at Ephesus, about "the spirit of wisdom and revelation in the knowledge of him." That prayer is about our mind's eye gaining insight into the true riches of the spirit. God is not giving us the spirit again. He is giving us wisdom in the knowledge of the spirit that He has already given to His sons (see Ephesians 1:16). The saint is to hold on to this spirit that God has given, for it is the proof of the unseen provisions of God. Utterance is one of the unseen riches of the spirit. We can bring it forth at any time because the spirit is the proof. Our feelings are expendable on this matter. Paying attention to feelings of inadequacy dulls the spiritual intelligence of the saint. Such feelings will perish but the spirit is forever.

19. Now therefore ye are no more strangers and foreigners, but fellowcitizens with the saints, and of the household of God; 20. And are built upon the foundation of the apostles and prophets, Jesus Christ himself being the chief corner stone; 21. In whom all the building fitly framed together groweth unto an holy temple

in the Lord: 22. In whom ye also are builded together for an habitation of God through the Spirit.
Ephesians 2: 19 - 22

God's plan is executed "through the Spirit." Each saint becomes the habitation of God through the spirit. This means that He inhabits the saint by the gift of His spirit within the saint. It is by that spirit that we belong in the family. We are of the household of God. All members of the family are the holy temple that God built.

15. But if I tarry long, that thou mayest know how thou oughtest to behave thyself in the house of God, which is the church of the living God, the pillar and ground of the truth.
1 Timothy 3: 15

Paul said the knowledge that we are the house of God should govern our behaviour. The Church of the living God is the ground and pillar of truth. Truth is reality or proof of that which is accomplished. The Church is the ground of truth because reality is found in the Church. The truth in the Church is the spirit of truth. The spirit that God has given to all saints as evidence that He has done all that He promised.

The acts of the spirit

The book of Acts is the historical record of the acts of the spirit in the saints.

2. And suddenly there came a sound from heaven as of a rushing mighty wind, and it filled all the house where they were sitting. 3. And there appeared unto them cloven tongues like as of fire, and it sat upon each of them. 4. And they were all filled with the Holy Ghost, and began to speak with other tongues, as the Spirit gave them utterance.
Acts 2: 2 - 4

Luke has recorded the experience of the saints the very first moments after they received the New Birth. Since they were freshly born again, these saints were in their default mode. Their default mode is the same as ours because we have the same salvation and the same Christ. Our sufficiency, as well as theirs, is of God who has made His saints able ministers. We cannot improve upon that; we can only improve upon our boldness to act on that fact. The major trouble of the saint is the temptation to abandon this default mode by trying to improve upon what God has done. In this default mode, without any spiritual growth, each of these new saints heard a heavenly sound and all saw a heavenly vision described as the cloven tongues of fire that appeared to all of them bar none. Each saint saw that vision enabled by the power of the New Birth as able ministers of the New Testament. This is the largest shared vision recorded in the bible.

Each man and woman acted on what the Lord had taught them for forty days (I believe He confirmed the fulfilment of His excellent teaching recorded in John 14 through 16). As they acted in faith, they saw visions and heard spiritual sounds. The Church was birthed in the opening up of the senses of the reborn spirit. These saints did not see visions, speak in tongues and interpret the same because there was any special power inherent in the day of Pentecost. The day of Pentecost was not the secret key to tongues, interpretation, visions and prophecy as well as every operation of the power of God in Acts 2. The spirit which the Lord Jesus has given to man as the New Birth is. He happened to give it on the day of Pentecost. Look past Pentecost and gaze on the spirit given.

The book of Acts records the supernatural events without explaining them. It is in the Epistles that we know what happened inside each saint. This gives to us an explanation of the actions of the spirit in Acts (see Ephesians 3:2-5).

15. What is it then? I will pray with the spirit, and I will pray with the understanding also: I will sing with the spirit, and I will sing with the understanding also.
1 Corinthians 14: 15

These men and women who had just seen visions and heard spiritual sounds opened their own mouth as an act of their will and spoke other sounds.

2. For he that speaketh in an unknown tongue speaketh not unto men, but unto God: for no man understandeth him; howbeit in the spirit he speaketh mysteries.
1 Corinthians 14: 2

Paul explains that the saints, by an act of their wills, can deliberately move their lips, tongue as well as push out sounds through the vocal chords to be "in the spirit." This means that the body and will of the saint are participating "in the spirit" whenever the saint performs the ordinary act of moving his or her mouth to speak out in other tongues.

On the Day of Pentecost, Luke presents speaking in tongues as the climax, while the seeing and hearing of spiritual things was the starting point! Ordinarily we'll expect to progress from tongues to visions. Since tongues is the climax, every saint that speaks in tongues proves that it is easy to see and hear in the spirit.

Seeing, knowing and speaking are characteristics of the spirit of the New Testament.

On earth and in heaven

This is what Paul said about the spirit:

14. For this cause I bow my knees unto the Father of our Lord Jesus Christ,
15. Of whom the whole family in heaven and earth is named,
Ephesians 3: 14 - 15

Paul bows his knee to the Father of the whole family. The family is in heaven and earth. It is not that some family members are on the earth and other members of that family are in heaven. What is said is that the family is at once on earth and in heaven. This is true of each member of the family. The body is on earth while the spirit is in heaven within the body. No, this does not mean that the spirit of man is omni-present. It means that the heavenlies have been made accessible to each saint in the New Birth. Everywhere the saint is, the spirit of the saint is in heaven on earth within the physical body. When saints fellowship together, we each bring forth something from the heavenlies by the spirit within. The assembly of the saints is the assembly of heavenlies.

5. Even when we were dead in sins, hath quickened us together with Christ, (by grace ye are saved;) 6. And hath raised us up together, and made us sit together in heavenly places in Christ Jesus:
Ephesians 2: 5 - 6

Paul repeatedly speaks of Christ, the saint, and the heavenly places. Although, the KJV says "heavenly places", the word "places" is always italicised. This means it was added by translators in each instance. So, Paul doesn't speak to the saints at Ephesus of heavenly places but heavenlies. His terminology tended to locate the heavenlies in Christ or in Christ Jesus. In either usage, the heavenlies are not geographic but the believer's status in Christ. Its meaning is that Christ is the heavenly sphere to the saint. In Christ Jesus, the saint already has all the heavenlies he or she would ever need (see also Ephesians 1:3). Paul has not used heavenlies in the way that we would have anticipated.

The New Birth is described as God having raised and placed us in the heavenlies in Christ. This placement in Christ is the translation of the saint into the kingdom of the Son. God does not stop at translation, the apostle declares that the saint then received the action of being sitted with Christ in the heavenlies in Christ. The spirit of man is sitted as Christ is sitted.

The writer of Hebrews says it this way:

22. But ye are come unto mount Sion, and unto the city of the living God, the heavenly Jerusalem, and to an innumerable company of angels, 23. To the general assembly and church of the firstborn, which are written in heaven, and to God the Judge of all, and to the spirits of just men made perfect, 24. And to Jesus the mediator of the new covenant, and to the blood of sprinkling, that

speaketh better things than that of Abel.
Hebrews 12: 22 - 24

Although, the writer mentions Mount Sion, there is no physical mountain. Neither is the city of the living God a reference to any literal city. By the same token, although the heavenly Jerusalem is mentioned, there is no Jerusalem in view. None of the things communicated are physical. They are all spiritual and therefore unseen. The writer says that the heavenly Jerusalem is the Church of the firstborn, which is the spirit of just men made perfect. This describes the saint in Christ.

55. But he, being full of the Holy Ghost, looked up stedfastly into heaven, and saw the glory of God, and Jesus standing on the right hand of God, 56. And said, Behold, I see the heavens opened, and the Son of man standing on the right hand of God. 57. Then they cried out with a loud voice, and stopped their ears, and ran upon him with one accord,
58. And cast him out of the city, and stoned him: and the witnesses laid down their clothes at a young man's feet, whose name was Saul. 59. And they stoned Stephen, calling upon God, and saying, Lord Jesus, receive my spirit.
Acts 7: 55 – 59

Luke shows that Stephen's secret was that he was full of the holy spirit. It was as one full of the spirit that Stephen looked up steadfastly into heaven, and saw the glory of God, and Jesus standing on the right hand of God. Stephen was deliberate. He lifted up his eyes and saw a vision. The things of the spirit involve the will of the saint. This fact is readily observable in the manifestation called tongues.

The spirit of the New Testament is the basis and proof of all things spiritual. Stephen was energised by the spirit to see the glory of God. Stephen saw glory in the heavenlies through his inward eyes. He spoke what he was seeing in the heavenlies. It was what he said from what he saw in that vision that stirred the mob to violence of stoning him.

Stephen was not yet dead when he saw Jesus. Therefore, his spirit was still within his body. His spirit was participating in heavenly things and giving Stephen's mind the experience of them in vision form. It is the same spirit that had manifested tongues that was manifesting visions.

The Lord Jesus had always been with Stephen's spirit in the heavenlies. The difference is that Stephen was speaking from a higher consciousness of the presence of Jesus. This is not about seeking experiences. It is cooperating with God who is working in us to do His good pleasure. The saint is to act based on the consciousness of God working in us by His spirit. The saint is to remember that God is already at work within by the spirit that He has given to the saint. In the New Testament, God does not work with a particular day, service, venue or event. His operation is in the saint. The blessings become manifest as the saint acts on the truth of what God has done.

The spirit of the New Testament is capable of tongues and visions as well as the expression of all that has to do with the glory of God.

John the beloved showed that each saint mingles with another world while still in a physical body.

> *9. I John, who also am your brother, and companion in tribulation, and in the kingdom and patience of Jesus Christ, was in the isle that is called Patmos, for the word of God, and for the testimony of Jesus Christ. 10. I was in the Spirit on the Lord's day, and heard behind me a great voice, as of a trumpet,*
> *Revelation 1: 9 - 10*

We already know that whenever the saint moves his or her mouth to speak out in other tongues by an act of the will, that saint is "in the spirit." So, when John said, "I was in the Spirit on the Lord's day", we expect that he had been speaking in tongues.

John had spoken in tongues until he became more conscious of the heavenlies. As a result, John entered into a deeper consciousness of the heavenly realm by yielding his will to his spirit. The spirit of the New Testament did not only cause him to speak and hear religious secrets in tongues, he also saw and sensed spiritual experiences. It wasn't physical death that had given John the rite of passage into another world by separating his body from his spirit. It is union with Christ via the reborn spirit within the physical body that opens man's spiritual faculties up as man yields his will to the spirit. John's heavenlies and "earthlies" were united. It is noteworthy that John's will was actively engaged throughout all this. John's experiences whet our appetite with regards to understanding the riches that the Lord has endowed the recreated human spirit with.

3

THE SPIRIT WHICH IS OF GOD

Paul taught the Corinthians about "the spirit which is of God".

12 Now we have received, not the spirit of the world, but the spirit which is of God; that we might know the things that are freely given to us of God.
1 Corinthians 2: 12

Paul is explaining the answer to the question "What spirit did we receive at the New Birth?"

Paul describes humanity in terms of spirit received. There are two options on offer - The spirit of the world or the spirit which is of God. Paul offers no other spirit aside these two. He wants you to know that if you have received one, then you do not possess the other. Paul shows that the opposite of the term "spirit which is of God" is the "spirit of the world". To say, "I have received the spirit which is of God", is to say "I have not received the spirit of the world". The term "spirit of the world" describes the sinner, while spirit which is of God describes the saint. He wants saints to know that we have not received the spirit of the world. What produces the New Birth is man receiving the spirit which is of God.

In Paul's pneumatology, the human spirit that is born again is the holy spirit which is of God. Unlike in the Old Testament, this holy spirit which we received at the New Birth is cell-for-cell part and parcel of the believer; thus, making him a brand-new creation. The saint is unlike anything gone before. We are truly a new species. This new spirit, which is a new nature has a real effect upon man in much the same way that the flesh influences a man. The primal effect of the gift of holy spirit in man is to bring about communion with God, accelerate spiritual insight and conform man to the image of Christ by renewing the mind. Since the holy spirit is not just a status of holiness but also of power, the influence of the holy spirit can be manifested as tremendous power.

Paul gave a test for knowing those that have received this spirit which is of God and God's gift in us:

3 Wherefore I give you to understand, that no man speaking by the Spirit of God calleth Jesus accursed: and that no man can say that Jesus is the Lord, but by the Holy Ghost.
1 Corinthians 12: 3

Paul was writing to saints that were familiar with the supernatural whom he had just informed, "I would not have you ignorant concerning the things of the spirit". When he says that it is by the Spirit of God that man confesses Jesus as Lord, Paul is re-stating the test for the New Birth in men and women.

What is meant by the Holy Ghost saying that Jesus is Lord?

The Father made Jesus both Lord and Christ. As to His confession, He says of the Lord Jesus, "thou art my Son" (see Hebrews 1:5). Therefore, the Father is not the Spirit that confesses, "Jesus is Lord". God is not the Holy Spirit that needs to call Jesus Lord.

Paul's point is that a man can only confess the Lordship of Jesus or receive the New Birth by the power from on high, the holy spirit, which Christ gives. The spirit that calls Jesus Lord is this holy spirit, which is God's divine nature and gift to man. By that confession, the spirit of man is created a new man in Christ. By extension, if the spirit of a man doesn't call Jesus Lord, then that fellow is not born again.

John gives the litmus test by which we can tell whether a spirit is of God or not:

1 Beloved, believe not every spirit, but try the spirits whether they are of God: because many false prophets are gone out into the world. 2 Hereby know ye the Spirit of God: Every spirit that confesseth that Jesus Christ is come in the flesh is of God: 3 And every spirit that confesseth not that Jesus Christ is come in the flesh is not of God: and this is that spirit of antichrist, whereof ye have heard that it should come; and even now already is it in the world. 4 Ye are of God, little children, and have overcome them: because greater is he that is in you, than he that is in the world.
1 John 4: 1 - 4

The false prophets function by the spirit of this world which John refers to as the antichrist spirit. Here, the antichrist spirit is not a Jewish man that will show up at the end of the age to rule the world. The antichrist is the spirit of unbelief in men and it is already in the world. John wants his readers to know how to test whether the human spirit is of God or of this world.

A man's spirit is of God when that spirit has confessed that Jesus is come in the flesh. If we harmonise this with the writings of Paul, this will be the same thing as confessing the Lordship of Jesus. Only the power from on high, the gift of holy spirit can call Jesus Lord. If the spirit of a man does not confess Jesus as Lord, then that spirit is of the world and not of God and such a man is anti-christ and a sinner.

Since the believers have confessed that Jesus is come in the flesh, which is the same thing as confessing the Lordship of Jesus, John assures them, "Ye are of God". Their confession of the Lordship of Christ was by the power from on high which birthed within them a new nature.

What does John mean by that term "he who is in the world"? "He who is in the world" refers to the nature of spiritual death in the first Adam. This is not a reference to the man Adam personally. Adam cannot be inside any other man for one man cannot be inside another man. This "he who is in the world" is man taking his place in the sin of unbelief, which is identification with Adam. Adam did not sin for anyone. Each man partakes of spiritual death, by rejecting the testimony of Jesus, which is refusal to confess that Jesus is come in the flesh. The spirit of the world is the human spirit in bondage to spiritual death.

That terminology "In you" or "within you" is shorthand which refers to the nature of a man.

Who is this greater one within?

Although, at first glance, we might be tempted to view this as a reference to Jesus, this is not the case. In the New Testament, Jesus is presented to us as our Mediator (see 1 Timothy 2:5). He is a man. Jesus cannot be within another human in much the same way that Adam cannot be within anyone else. Thus, frankly speaking, Jesus is not within the saint. The greater one within is His nature that He has given as the gift of the holy spirit, which becomes the new nature in man. This is what Paul would call "Christ in you".

This greater one within refers to the greater work of the new nature within the saint. It is referred to as "greater one" in contrast to "he that is in the world", which is spiritual death. John refers to the gift of holy spirit, which is the power from on high within the saint as "the greater one". This term means that by confessing the lordship of Jesus and receiving His nature, the born-again spirit has overcome the spiritual death that held the spirit of man in bondage. This greater one within is the born-again spirit that is of God.

So, if we harmonise John and Paul, we see that John's "he that is in the world" is none other than Paul's the "spirit of this world".

Furthermore, John's "greater is he who is in you" is none other than Paul's the "spirit which is of God".

Once we have received the spirit which is of God, our bodies become the temple of the recreated spirit, which is of God (see 1 Corinthians 6:19).

Paul reminded the Galatians of the central truth of how receiving the spirit relates to salvation:

1 O foolish Galatians, who hath bewitched you, that ye should not obey the truth, before whose eyes Jesus Christ hath been evidently set forth, crucified among you? 2 This only would I learn of you, Received ye the Spirit by the works of the law, or by the hearing of faith?
Galatians 3: 1 - 2

Firstly, the Greek word translated as the term "hath been evidently set" is translated in other places, as "written beforehand" (see Romans 15:4) and "written before" (see Ephesians 3:3). So, what Paul said could be translated as,

"...who hath bewitched you, that ye should not obey the truth, before whose eyes Jesus Christ hath been written beforehand as crucified among you."

That which had been written before refers to the things written in the prophetic scriptures about Christ. He was saying that the prophetic scriptures had painted a clear picture of the sufferings of Christ (see Acts 26:22-23). Paul had preached the Gospel by using the prophetic scriptures to show Christ's suffering.

As a side note, Paul himself had admitted that he was untrained in speech and that he was not an eloquent speaker (see 2 Corinthians 11:5-6 and 2 Corinthians 10:10). Therefore, that expression, "before whose eyes Jesus Christ hath been evidently set forth, crucified among you", could not be saying that Paul was so eloquent in his presentation of the Gospel that it was like showing the Galatians a cinema that transported them to front row seats at Calvary.

Faith was contained within Paul's preaching of the sufferings of Christ according to scriptures. As a result of this, the Galatians had received eternal life. Instead of asking them "How did you receive the New Birth?", Paul used the more technical term, "Received ye the Spirit by the works of the law, or by the hearing of faith?"

This spirit that they received was the gift given. They had received that spirit by believing the Gospel. Therefore, the New Birth is receiving the gift of a new spirit from the Lord. In this verse, "Spirit" refers to the gift given and not the Giver of that gift.

Letting the spirit transform our walk

Paul used this fact that the saints at Corinth had received the spirit to correct them when they were acting in a worldly manner.

16 Know ye not that ye are the temple of God, and that the Spirit of God dwelleth in you?
1 Corinthians 3: 16

God's holiness does not make Him shield Himself from sinful men, aggressively sanitizing Himself anytime He comes in contact with them. We know His holiness does not contain those ideas because He chose Judas, a sinful man as His ministry partner, He ate in the house of Zacchaeus the sinner and stayed for nine months in the womb of Mary. In fact, God did not reserve the term "holy" for Himself in the bible. Anything that God sets apart is holy. This is true of both lifeless and living things. For this reason, under the shadow, the ground on which Moses stood, Aaron's crown, the altar, all the vessels of the tabernacle, as well as all the meat offerings and sin offerings were all declared holy or most holy (see Exodus 3:5; 29:6; 40:9-10, Leviticus 6:16-25). Since none of these things can have character or produce actions, we see that a thing is holy or most holy apart from its character and only because God says that it is.

All that God called holy or most holy are shadows or copies of the true tabernacle (see Hebrews 8:5). In admitting that the shadow is most holy, we humbly affirm that the spirit, which is the reality possessed in Christ is the holiest of all. We are the true and heavenly tabernacle created in Christ Jesus without human hands.

We are the temple of God.

Paul does not reason like we do today. We would have said that by acting like carnal men and women they established that they did not have the spirit of God. Paul's point was that the Church at Corinth, as a collective, formed a habitation for God because the spirit of God indwelt each saint at Corinth.

Paul did not say, "Know ye not that ye are the temple of God, and that the Spirit of God dwelleth in all of you except those who are new Christians who do not yet speak in tongues".

Paul could not find a single saint at Corinth that was not indwelt of the spirit of God, including those who just got born again. Paul's assertion is that the indwelling of the spirit is common to all. In which case, it is at the moment of the New Birth that the spirit of God comes to indwell man. Thus, we do not receive the spirit after salvation but at salvation and as salvation. Translators should not have capitalised "Spirit" in that verse. The reception of a new spirit is the New Birth. Salvation is not different from receiving the spirit as gift. We don't get saved one day and then receive the spirit later in our walk when some Pentecostal crosses our path and teaches us about Acts 2. In fact, salvation is receiving a new spirit, the spirit which is of God, within us. That spirit is eternal life.

Then as we yield to the spirit, through the Word that spirit becomes our style. This is what births the lifestyle. It is the style of the spirit through the implanted Word. It is the consciousness of the spirit through the Word that shapes our walk.

If this knowledge of divine capacity via the indwelling spirit is lacking in us, we'll find that we have robbed ourselves of the transforming power of the spirit of God which is the gift that our Father God gives us. This holy spirit is God's gift of His nature to man and the primary reason for receiving the gift of holy spirit from God is that it is our means of spirit-to-Spirit communion with God. That new nature by its character, also contains the ability to so transform our walk that it conforms our walk to the image of Christ within as we yield to its influence.

God has given the spirit as life and power to the saint. The saint is to let the knowledge of that life produce lifestyle through the Word. Life and lifestyle must not be confused. We do not base our truths on people's flaws, personalities or whims; we base it on the Word. Although, all saints have life via the spirit of God, sadly not all would manifest the style associated with being indwelt by God's spirit.

Through the New Birth, Christ has made the saint holy by giving the promised spirit as the climax of His finished works. The reception of the promised spirit is the reception of holiness of the highest grade once and for all time. Since God is holy, that which is born of God is also holy. The New Birth makes the saint permanently holy for that is all that God is. This is God's amazing gift to every man who believes that God raised Jesus from the dead. God's plan of salvation makes the Christian a holy spirit.

Thus, we must not think that the terms "holy" and "spirit" are exclusively for God since the terms "holy" and "spirit" are equally true of God, who is the Giver, and His saints who are recipients. God as Giver is Holy Spirit while the saint as recipient is holy spirit. God gives the holy spirit (actually it is most times more accurate to say, "God gives holy spirit"). The spirit that is severally spoken of in the New Testament as the gift, the infilling, the baptism or the falling upon is the holy spirit which is God's gift. The Giver and His gift are so alike that only careful study of the Word shows us the difference.

Christ in you

2 If ye have heard of the dispensation of the grace of God which is given me to you-ward: 3 How that by revelation he made known unto me the mystery; (as I wrote afore in few words, 4 Whereby, when ye read, ye may understand my

knowledge in the mystery of Christ)
Ephesians 3: 2 - 4

The word that Paul used for "mystery" does not mean just any type of secret. It is specifically a religious secret. Paul told the Corinthians that this religious secret was hidden from the view of satan and the rulers and that it was for our glory (see 1 Corinthians 2:7). The mystery of Christ is the revelation of redemption and righteousness in Christ Jesus by the supply of a new spirit in man, by which man partakes of the divine nature. In his writings, the Apostle Paul faithfully recorded his understanding of the mystery of Christ. To the Colossians, Paul summarised this mystery as "Christ in you the hope of glory".

27 To whom God would make known what is the riches of the glory of this mystery among the Gentiles; which is Christ in you, the hope of glory
Colossians 1: 27

The glory spoken of refers to a glorified body. This is why it is referred to as a hope. Notice that the terminology is Christ in you and not Jesus in you. Jesus is the person. Sometimes He is called Jesus Christ and other times Christ Jesus. These are not flippant terms. They are pregnant with meaning.

The word "Christ" describes Jesus as the one who is anointed with the spirit, which is the power of God (see Acts 10:38). Jesus received this spirit in a unique way - without measure (see John 3:34). It was as Christ or the one enabled with holy spirit that He executed the plan of redemption. Christ is not His person but His work as Redeemer.

Therefore, "Christ in you", is not the person of Jesus. It means that the saint also carries that spirit without measure as a son of God. This is the high note of triumph in God–The Lord Jesus has given you the enabling holy spirit "without measure" as a son of God – just as it was given to Jesus. The heart of Paul's knowledge in the mystery of Christ is the understanding of the gift of holy spirit in the saint.

In the Epistles we find that God has given the saint only one thing - the spirit. The spirit is eternal life and redemption, which is the forgiveness of sins. This spirit, which we sometimes refer to as the recreated human spirit, is the seal, the promise, the power from on high, the anointing, the earnest and the guarantee. The spirit is the very holiness and power of God in the New Birth. That spirit is the status of power and holiness in Christ and it makes the saint as holy as God. The spirit in Christ is our assurance that a glorified body is inevitable.

Within Paul's documentation of his understanding of the mystery of Christ, we find that Paul amplifies our understanding of the spirit of man by describing it in the light of what Christ has accomplished. Paul's message, "Christ in you" is an unfolding of his amplified pneumatology. I firmly believe that we can only properly understand the spirit of man via the revelation of Christ. A careful study of the Word leads me to conclude that our Christology shapes our pneumatology. Paul's teaching of the unsearchable riches of Christ invariably contains various descriptions of the spirit of man. It is a thrilling fact that we do not have to become mystics or magicians in order to understand the things of the recreated spirit since they are birthed, explained and sustained by the revelation of the riches of Christ through the Word. God's Word is our sure foundation.

The gift and its manifestation

In spite of his faithfulness to record his understanding of the mystery of Christ, much of Paul's phenomenal, first-class treatment of the spirit of man is little understood today.

1 Now concerning spiritual gifts, brethren, I would not have you ignorant.
1 Corinthians 12: 1

It is noteworthy that the term "the gifts of the spirit" cannot be found in the bible until we come into Paul's Epistles. It is in his revelation of the mystery that we find rich insights into the spirit and our pneumatology finds its proper footing in Christ.

Our translators have used gift and spiritual together thus creating and inserting the idea of "spiritual gifts" in our unsuspecting minds, when the text says no such thing. There is no single word in that verse which can be translated as gifts. Scholars have pointed out that the Greek word charisma, which means gift and the Greek word 'Pneumatikos', only ever occur once together in all of the New Testament. This fact is not obvious if you do not have a good bible translation. Our translations make it look like they occur together. Thus, the idea of "spiritual gifts" is deeply embedded in the subconscious of the Pentecostal and it is a sacred cow that does not die easily. It came as a shock to my Pentecostal mind-set the first time it was pointed out to me that the term "the gifts of the Spirit" is not exactly used in the bible – It still shocks many lovers of God's Word today. True, there are many modern bible translations that use the term but you won't find it in the Greek.

The KJV does a good job of italicising gifts when used in proximity to the word spirit. This lets us know that the word "gifts" is an addition by the translators. The Greek word which is there is 'pneumatikos' and it means "that which pertains to the spirit".

In his letters to the Corinthians, Paul wrote about the "manifestation of the spirit". Not taking note of these distinctions between the gift and its manifestation, we often speak of the gifts thus losing sight of the fact that the gift is the holy spirit, which makes us saints in the New Birth. We often say gifts when we mean to say manifestation. This is not just semantics. If we treat a manifestation as a gift, we'll muddle up the clarity supplied by God's Word and this will show up in our practice of the supernatural. The new spirit, which is Eternal Life, is a gift. The various ministries of teacher, evangelist or prophet are also gifts.

However, prophecy, tongues and interpretation of tongues which we call gifts of the spirit are all manifestations and not gifts. We manifest something that we already have, whereas we await the giving of a gift. We get a gift when another person gives it to us and until that other person gives the gift you do not have it. Every saint has the gift of holy spirit but the vast majority do not manifest it as prophecy, tongues and interpretation of tongues. Gifts come from God whereas manifestations come from the gift of holy spirit. Manifestation means that the gift is given and God is waiting on you – the next move is yours.

To stay biblical, we should be referring to the term "manifestation of the spirit" rather than gifts of the spirit. We are not looking for gifts; for the gift that the New Testament majors on is the promise of the ages, the gift of holy spirit. In order to manifest the gift of spirit, we must have been recipients of holy spirit through the New Birth.

Let us observe once again Luke's summary of what the Lord Jesus taught His disciples for forty days before He ascended to sit at God's right hand.

8 But ye shall receive power, after that the Holy Ghost is come upon you: and ye shall be witnesses unto me both in Jerusalem, and in all Judaea, and in Samaria, and unto the uttermost part of the earth.
Acts 1: 8

Some other translations render this verse as, "ye shall receive power, when the Holy Ghost is come upon you". This helps us see that the power from on high that God promised upon man is received when we receive the holy spirit at the New Birth itself and not afterwards. The Lord Jesus was particular about this fact that the spirit of God upon man is accompanied with tremendous power. When one believes on the Lord, he or she, once and for all time, receives the spirit, which is the same thing as receiving the power of God in fullness. The capacity received by all saints is the same since there is one Giver and one spirit given as gift to all. However, the measure manifested by each saint varies based on several factors. Once we receive the spirit it is our responsibility to receive, lay hold on or recognise the spirit as power. Thus, we find that all that have the gift of holy spirit can manifest the holy spirit as power.

Paul then lists the various categorizations of this manifestation:

8 For to one is given by the Spirit the word of wisdom; to another the word of knowledge by the same Spirit; 9 To another faith by the same Spirit; to another

the gifts of healing by the same Spirit; 10 To another the working of miracles; to another prophecy; to another discerning of spirits; to another divers kinds of tongues; to another the interpretation of tongues
1 Corinthians 12: 8 – 10

In verse 8, we see the phrases "given by the Spirit" and "by the same Spirit". Then in verse 9, we have "by the same Spirit" twice. Without a doubt, Paul's emphasis is that the spirit is the agenct. God's gift of holy spirit gives all of the manifestations that are listed here. The implication is that all that have the holy spirit have the various abilities listed here.

Another way of saying it is that there are nine ways to manifest the one gift of holy spirit. The Lord Jesus exerts a marvellous impact through His gift of holy spirit in the Christian.

Observe that of this list of nine manifestations, there are two that announce the glorification of Christ in His sitting at the right hand of God at the commencement of the Church. No one who was saved prior to the sitting of Christ ever had these two manifestations of tongues and the interpretation of tongues. They could not because Christ was not glorified. Christ could not be glorified until He sat down at God's right hand.

So, although David was saved and could prophesy because he had the spirit upon him, since Christ was not exalted at that point in time, David never had the holy spirit as we have it today; therefore, he wasn't a new creation while he walked this earth. For this reason, David could never manifest tongues. In the Church, we have God's precious gift given to us in a way that it had never been given to man.

Today, we can manifest that spirit by speaking utterances in the form of tongues and interpretation of tongues because Christ is seated and sonship is provided through the New Birth permanently and unconditionally. The twin manifestations of tongues and interpretation of tongues are the unique and authentic witnesses that man's spirit has been permanently made the son of God on the basis of what Christ has done.

11 And this is the record, that God hath given to us eternal life, and this life is in his Son.
1 John 5: 11

John's meaning is more obvious if we remove that comma between "record" and "that" (Hey! There was no comma in the Greek, so relax we are not changing God's Word. We are changing our thinking).

It should then read this way: And this is the record that God hath given to us eternal life, and this life is in his Son. We can give of His witness within us to our world in the form of manifestation. We are enabled to manifest that spirit which we have received of God. No saint alive today needs go to Jerusalem to point out an empty tomb as proof of His resurrection. We have a living union with the ascended Lord, by which we show that He is alive. The spirit that we manifest is proof of His resurrection.

24 And he that keepeth his commandments dwelleth in him, and he in him. And hereby we know that he abideth in us, by the Spirit which he hath given us.
1 John 3: 24

The gift of holy spirit that we received from God at the New Birth is intangible in the same way that God is intangible to our touch.

How then do we show that He abides in us?

To show that we have received the spirit, we manifest some characteristics of that intangible spirit. The intangible spirit that we received from the Lord Jesus carries with it the power and the right for manifestations in the form of the love walk, the desire for truth, spiritual development and the ability to comprehend God's communication to us. All these are imprints of this spirit. In addition, we have the power and the right to manifest this intangible spirit which is of God by speaking in tongues.

God has deposited His riches within His gift to us, which is the promise of God and the power from on high. All the riches are in the spirit and all saints have this spirit as earnest and within that earnest is an enablement to manifest the riches that God has to us. Therefore, there are no ungifted Christians. It is simply not true that some saints are gifted and others are not. The gift of holy spirit came at great cost to the Father.

Do not be afraid. Recognise and activate God's gift in you today.

4

THE MINISTRY OF THE SPIRIT

Before He ascended to the Father's right hand, Jesus taught His disciples to wait in Jerusalem for the promise of the spirit. The idea of the spirit resting upon men finds precedence in the Old Testament. However, the Lord Jesus puts a twist on this narrative by informing His disciples that He, as the resurrected Lord, was the one sending the promised spirit upon them in Jerusalem.

49 And, behold, I send the promise of my Father upon you: but tarry ye in the city of Jerusalem, until ye be endued with power from on high.
Luke 24: 49

Jesus referred to this promise of the spirit as being clothed with power from on high, which is the same thing as being born again or being born from above. The holy spirit that we receive at the New Birth is the power of God in us.

8 But ye shall receive power, after that the Holy Ghost is come upon you: and ye shall be witnesses unto me both in Jerusalem, and in all Judaea, and in Samaria, and unto the uttermost part of the earth.
Acts 1: 8

It is at the New Birth itself, and not afterwards, that we receive the holy spirit as the promised power from on high.

What the Lord Jesus said about the gift of the holy spirit being the power from on high jives with the fact that all those that had the spirit of God upon them in the Old Testament manifested tremendous power.

16 And the LORD said unto Moses, Gather unto me seventy men of the elders of Israel, whom thou knowest to be the elders of the people, and officers over them; and bring them unto the tabernacle of the congregation, that they may stand there with thee.17 And I will come down and talk with thee there: and I will take of the spirit which is upon thee, and will put it upon them; and they shall bear the burden of the people with thee, that thou bear it not thyself alone.
Numbers 11: 16 - 17

God is the Giver who had put His spirit upon Moses. Moses then used the spirit that was placed upon him by God, to carry out the task of government.

It is important to note that although some of these seventy leaders might be saved, none of them had the spirit initially. Prior to Jesus' sitting at God's right hand, the vast majority of people who were saved were not given the spirit. Salvation and receiving the spirit were not one and the same.

It was when the demand of Moses' office became too much, that God took of that spirit which was upon Moses and gave it as a gift upon the seventy. Even though God gave the seventy the gift of spirit, the rest of the millions of Jews, whether saved or not, were not given that spirit. It was only after God had put the spirit upon the seventy that they could hear God and perform those superhuman feats. As a result, these seventy then governed in a higher capacity than before. The gift of spirit imparted capacity and ability.

The spirit is ability to prophesy

25 And the LORD came down in a cloud, and spake unto him, and took of the spirit that was upon him, and gave it unto the seventy elders: and it came to pass, that, when the spirit rested upon them, they prophesied, and did not cease.
Numbers 11: 25

Notice that although Moses had the spirit upon him, he could not give the spirit to another. God is the Giver who put His spirit upon the seventy also.

Moses testified that as a result of the gift of spirit resting upon these seventy, they were not only enabled to be better administrators, they also acquired the ability to prophesy. Although the KJV says, "they prophesied, and did not cease", other translations like the NIV render it as, "they prophesied—but did not do so again". So, we see that in the Old Testament when people had the holy spirit upon them, its effect was not permanent. These elders prophesied only once. Thus, in the Old Testament, they had the spirit in a conditional and temporary way; even then, they could prophesy.

God has always been the Giver of the spirit and when the holy spirit is upon people, they prophesy.

18 Then the spirit came upon Amasai, who was chief of the captains, and he said, Thine are we, David, and on thy side, thou son of Jesse: peace, peace be unto thee, and peace be to thine helpers; for thy God helpeth thee. Then David received them, and made them captains of the band.
1 Chronicles 12: 18

According to the NIV, the words that Amasai spoke to David when the spirit came upon him were, "We are yours, David! We are with you, son of Jesse! Success, success to you, and success to those who help you, for your God will help you." Amasai ministered a prophecy assuring David of success.

41 And it came to pass, that, when Elisabeth heard the salutation of Mary, the babe leaped in her womb; and Elisabeth was filled with the Holy Ghost:42 And

she spake out with a loud voice, and said, Blessed art thou among women, and blessed is the fruit of thy womb.
Luke 1: 41 – 42

John the Baptist's mother, Elizabeth, prophesied because of the holy spirit.

67 And his father Zacharias was filled with the Holy Ghost, and prophesied,
saying, 68 Blessed be the Lord God of Israel; for he hath visited and redeemed
his people,
Luke 1: 67 - 68

John the Baptist's father, Zechariah, prophesied because of the holy spirit.

35 And the angel answered and said unto her, The Holy Ghost shall come upon
thee, and the power of the Highest shall overshadow thee: therefore also that holy
thing which shall be born of thee shall be called the Son of God. 46 And Mary
said, My soul doth magnify the Lord, 47 And my spirit hath rejoiced in God
my Saviour.
Luke 1: 35, 46 – 47

One of the effects of the overshadowing of the Spirit on Mary was that she also prophesied.

38 How God anointed Jesus of Nazareth with the Holy Ghost and with power: who went about doing good, and healing all that were oppressed of the devil; for God was with him.
Acts 10:38

Notice that God was also the Giver of the spirit, even to Jesus.

God did not give Jesus two things – spirit and power. The power further explained the holy spirit that God had given Jesus. What God gave Jesus was the gift of holy spirit, which was spiritual power. Unlike all others before Him, God gave Jesus the spirit without measure (see John 3:34). The big point is that it was when God gave the gift of His spirit to Jesus that Jesus became spiritually empowered to commence

His ministry, as a result of which Jesus also prophesied. From then on, Jesus executed His task with that power.

33 Therefore being by the right hand of God exalted, and having received of the Father the promise of the Holy Ghost, he hath shed forth this, which ye now see and hear.
Acts 2: 33

The Father has exalted the Lord Jesus to such an extent that it is the Lord Jesus who is the Giver of the spirit today.

In keeping with scriptural pattern, when anyone receives the spirit of God permanently in the New Birth, there is power in his or her life. Since the spirit showed up in the seventy as ability to prophesy, then we'll perfectly expect that the saint in the New Testament receives, through the holy spirit at the New Birth, in a forever way, the ability to prophesy and more distinctly the ability to respond to utterance by speaking in tongues.

6 And when Paul had laid his hands upon them, the Holy Ghost came on them; and they spake with tongues, and prophesied.
Acts 19: 6

We observe that, just as the gift of spirit enabled men to prophesy prior to Jesus' exaltation, we see a continuation of this pattern afterwards. When the holy spirit came upon the saints at Ephesus, they spoke in tongues and prophesied. Speaking in tongues is peculiar to the Church age. Although, the bible warns about false prophets and false prophecies, the Bible never warns us about false tongues.

Does the account of Phillip's ministry in Samaria teach that men and women received the Holy Spirit subsequent to becoming born again?

14 Now when the apostles which were at Jerusalem heard that Samaria had received the word of God, they sent unto them Peter and John: 15 Who, when they were come down, prayed for them, that they might receive the Holy Ghost: 16 For as yet he was fallen upon none of them: only they were baptized in the name of the Lord Jesus.) 17 Then laid they their hands on them, and they

received the Holy Ghost.
Acts 8: 14 - 17

Samaria had received the Word of God. Phillip knew it. The Apostles at Jerusalem knew it and the Samaritans knew it. That word "received" in "heard that Samaria had received the word of God", means that the people of Samaria had warmed up to Philip's ministry by accepting the Word that he had preached to them.

We then observe that Peter and John came down and prayed for the Samaritans that they might receive the Holy Ghost. The Holy Ghost, which was to be received is the gift of God. Therefore, they were to receive holy spirit and not Holy Spirit.

Notice that although both verse fourteen and fifteen focus on "receive", the word translated receive in verse fourteen is totally different from the word translated receive in verse fifteen. This means that these Samaritans were not receiving in verse fifteen in the same sense that they had received in verse fourteen. So, we must not conclude that although the Samaritans had received the Word, they had not received the spirit if by that we mean that they had the Word but not the spirit!

The fact that the Samaritans "had not received the holy ghost" meant that they had not taken the initiative of receiving holy spirit. It is as though they were waiting for something to push them. Since they were born again, these saints already had the holy spirit but they had not taken any action that you would expect from someone that had the spirit. They had not done what Peter and John had done on the day of Pentecost – they had not begun to speak. They were waiting for something when they should have manifested on the outside, the spirit that was already within them in the New Birth. The manifesting is the taking (or receiving). The point at which they manifested the spirit must not be confused with when they received the gift of holy spirit. These saints were to receive the holy spirit, by recognising the spirit's presence and power.

Manifesting the anointing

4 Now there are diversities of gifts, but the same Spirit. 5 And there are differences of administrations, but the same Lord. 6 And there are diversities of operations, but it is the same God which worketh all in all.
7But the manifestation of the Spirit is given to every man to profit withal.
1 Corinthians 12: 4 - 7

Paul teaches that God energises us. The word "worketh" conveys the idea of plugging into the flow of power. We like to call that flow of power the "anointing" but Paul calls it "working"; therefore, so as not to confuse ourselves, we should endeavour to use bible terms to describe biblical things. The anointing is the gift of spirit that God has given to all saints. So, all saints are anointed but we sense His energising differently at different times.

Notice that in verses 4 - 6, Paul is looking at things from the God-side. The God-side can be summarised by the word "diversities," which refer to that which God distributes via the spirit. Then in verse 7, he focuses on that which is in the domain of each saint. He calls this manifestation. He has switched from talking about distributions to talking about manifestation.

The gift of holy spirit is invisible and intangible for it is of God, who is invisible and outside the domain of the senses. We are to manifest this invisible holy spirit by taking action on the revelations that we receive from the Lord through the spirit. Manifestation is a very important concept to understand.

Linguists tell us that our English word "manifestation" is the joining together of two Latin words - manus, which means "hand," and festare, which means "to touch". Therefore, manifestation means to make tangible. Manifestation means that we are making tangible to the senses that which we already have spiritually. Thus, we see that manifestation and gift are two different concepts. To prove that we have received the gift of holy spirit, we can manifest some characteristics of the spirit. Manifestation puts the ball in your court. What are you doing with the divine deposit?

While the saint is not responsible for distributions, he or she is responsible for manifestation of the spirit that God has given. God gives and the saint manifests. The saint chooses to manifest or not manifest the spirit. However, through His Word, the Lord has given direction on what is acceptable and not acceptable when saints manifest the spirit. He also does this by directly instructing the saint through the gift of holy spirit in a given situation.

8 For to one is given by the Spirit the word of wisdom; to another the word of knowledge by the same Spirit; 9To another faith by the same Spirit; to another the gifts of healing by the same Spirit; 10 To another the working of miracles; to another prophecy; to another discerning of spirits; to another divers kinds of tongues; to another the interpretation of tongues:
1 Corinthians 12: 8 – 10

In the Greek of this text, Paul uses two different words for "another". One of the two words translated as another, means "of the same kind" and the other word means "of a different kind". Paul places the word of wisdom and the word of knowledge together for they are of the same kind. Then he states that gift of faith, gifts of healing, working of miracles, prophecy and discerning of spirits are another group which are of a different kind to the word of wisdom and word of knowledge but same kind to one another. Lastly, he puts tongues and interpretation of tongues in a class by themselves and states that they are of the same kind to one another but different to all else.

Tongues and interpretation of tongues are distinctive of the New Testament. It makes sense that tongues and interpretation of tongues are in their own special category since the manifestation of tongues and interpretation of tongues never occurred in the Old Testament. People that had the spirit upon them prophesied but they never spoke in tongues. Since they never spoke in tongues, they could never have interpreted it. God does not give the ability to speak in tongues or to interpret tongues separate from salvation and righteousness. He gives the spirit and within the gift of holy spirit is the ability to manifest tongues as well as interpretation of tongues. These characteristics are supplied because of the sitting and glorification of Christ at God's right hand.

When we read "For to one is given by the Spirit the word of wisdom; to another the word of knowledge by the same Spirit", the words "to one" and "to another" appear to promote the idea that these things of the spirit are in some saints but not in others.

The Old Testament mind-set that supposes that some are gifted while some are not, causes us to read the verses as,

To one is given by the Spirit, prophecy.

To another is given by the Spirit, divers kinds of tongues.

To yet another is given by the Spirit, the interpretation of tongues.

Reading it that way does not jive with Paul's commands. That mind-set is at odds with Paul's commands in the two chapters of 1 Corinthians 12 and 1 Corinthians 14.

We must resolve the seeming contradiction.

Paul clearly told the same Corinthians,

5 I would that ye all spake with tongues, but rather that ye prophesied: for greater is he that prophesieth than he that speaketh with tongues, except he interpret, that the church may receive edifying.31 For ye may all prophesy one by one, that all may learn, and all may be comforted.
1 Corinthians 14: 5, 31

These instructions make no sense if Paul was teaching that it is only a select few that are given prophecy by the spirit. The fact that he expected all saints to speak with tongues invalidates any attempt to read, "To one is given by the Spirit divers kinds of tongues" to mean that only certain individuals are given the diversities of tongues. When we read it in a way that makes diversities of tongues exclusive to some people and not to all saints, we make tongues a gift. By extension, prophecy would also be a gift. This is how we end up with many gifts. Neither tongues nor prophesying are the gift – the gift is the one spirit that Christ gives to all saints.

When Paul said to the saints, "I would that ye all spake with tongues, but rather that ye prophesied", he meant that all saints had these abilities. If Paul meant that there is a gift of prophecy which is given only to certain individuals, why would he tell all believers to covet to prophesy?

Here's Peter's testimony:

16 But this is that which was spoken by the prophet Joel; 17 And it shall come to pass in the last days, saith God, I will pour out of my Spirit upon all flesh: and your sons and your daughters shall prophesy, and your young men shall see visions, and your old men shall dream dreams:
18 And on my servants and on my handmaidens I will pour out in those days of my Spirit; and they shall prophesy:
Acts 2: 16 - 18

Peter quoted Joel at Pentecost and Joel's prophecy said that the spirit would be poured on all flesh, as a result of which sons and daughters would prophesy. Peter implies that all the flesh that the spirit is poured on would prophesy. This confirms that the gift of holy spirit is the ability to prophesy. Additionally, it shows that this ability is available to all saints and not a select few.

A plain reading of Peter's preaching, Joel's prophecy and Paul's instructions would lead us to say that prophecy is the manifestation of the outpoured spirit on all saints.

A slight adjustment is needed in our thinking. We should not think of prophecy as a gift. Instead, we should think of it as the manifestation of the recreated human spirit which is of God. That adjustment helps us appreciate that Paul's commands to the saints to prophesy are not to be taken as suggestions but as the express commands of the Lord. He has commanded it because we have been given the enablement through His gift of holy spirit to us.

Paul is saying in effect, since you have the spirit, you should follow through with prophecy. Thus, we prophesy as a way of manifesting the spirit that God has given us.

The pattern from the book of Acts is that as soon as a man believes that God raised Jesus from the dead, he receives the gift of a new spirit from the Lord Jesus and the ability to manifest the gift of that spirit in utterance. The Lord gives the utterance, then the spirit gives that utterance to the will and the saint then speaks it out. Thus, the manifestation of speaking in tongues is real time communion between each saint and the risen Lord.

Paul's instructions in 1 Corinthians 14 helps us see that manifesting the holy spirit by speaking in tongues is under the control of the saint speaking in tongues. It is because the manifestation is under the speaker's control, and therefore subject to abuse and misuse that Paul uses a whole chapter to give instructions on the proper administration of manifestations of the spirit. He is telling the saints, "Hey! This is how to do it properly". It is possible that when we start out on this journey, we might manifest the spirit improperly. We let Paul's instructions fine tune our practice.

5 Not that we are sufficient of ourselves to think any thing as of ourselves; but
our sufficiency is of God; 6 Who also hath made us able ministers of the new
testament; not of the letter, but of the spirit: for the letter killeth, but the spirit
giveth life. 7 But if the ministration of death, written and engraven in stones,
was glorious, so that the children of Israel could not stedfastly behold the face of
Moses for the glory of his countenance; which glory was to be done away: 8 How
shall not the ministration of the spirit be rather glorious?
2 Corinthians 3: 5 - 8

The New Covenant deals with life and not death. Therefore it wasn't ratified by the death of Jesus but by the resurrection of Christ.

Every single saint has already been made sufficient by God. This sufficiency has been given to each saint as the spirit that made us saints. The peculiarity of the New Testament is that no saint occupies the room of a spectator who stands by while other "special" cadre of saints manifest the spirit. God Himself has qualified each saint to manifest that divine sufficiency today by the manifestation of the spirit. There are no saints who are not qualified or unable to minister the same spirit. The New Testament is the ministration of the spirit.

There is no condemnation or death in the ministration of the spirit. It has to do with life. There is no death in it.

Paul's understanding of the finished works of Christ showed up in his phenomenal pneumatology over and over again. The spirit occupies a central place in the New Testament. It is in understanding Christ that we get an explanation of this spirit, which is the distinctive of the finished works of Christ. We can only properly comprehend the born again spirit in Christ, for our pneumatology is shaped by our Christology.

All births, whether spiritual or natural only happen once. Since the giving of the spirit is a birth, we understand that God does not give the spirit again and again. God only gives the spirit once. He does not give the spirit every time the supernatural is in demonstration and manifestation. The saint is filled to full measure or full capacity at the New Birth. As saints we recognise that we have been enabled by God; therefore, it is up to us saints to take our place in the New Covenant by yielding to the influence of the spirit.

Here's what Paul says while describing the things of the spirit of a born again one:

4 Now there are diversities of gifts, but the same Spirit. 5 And there are differences of administrations, but the same Lord. 6 And there are diversities of operations, but it is the same God which worketh all in all.
1 Corinthians 12: 4 - 6

We must not to ignorant about the fact that the gift of holy spirit that the Lord Jesus gave to man can be variously expressed as manifestations, as ministries and as operations.

We energize God's gift to us into manifestation when we exercise faith in the influence of the spirit. We run into trouble when we look away from the Word and try to explain spiritual manifestations from the natural standpoint. It is not the Holy Spirit, the Giver that comes and goes in our meetings. We fluctuate in responding to the gift of God. The manifest presence of God fluctuates in "strength" because the permanent gift of holy spirit, which is God's nature in the saint, is not always acted upon. When acted upon, we have manifestations. When faith is not exercised, there is no energizing.

Rather than heed God's Word and manifest the spirit as able ministers of the New Testament, many pray for the Holy Spirit to attend their meetings. Such reasoning, praying and believing reveals that the saints are waiting for the Holy Spirit to move them, whereas according to God's Word, God expects the saints to desire spiritual manifestations by utilizing the holy spirit that all saints have been given as a gift at the disposal of the saint to be used for His glory.

Joel's prophecy has been fulfilled

17 And it shall come to pass in the last days, saith God, I will pour out of my Spirit upon all flesh: and your sons and your daughters shall prophesy, and your young men shall see visions, and your old men shall dream dreams: 18 And on my servants and on my handmaidens I will pour out in those days of my Spirit; and they shall prophesy
Acts 2:17 - 18

Peter's sermon at Pentecost lifted the veil on Joel's prophecy by letting us see that God is the promise keeper pouring out or giving the holy spirit. Therefore, God is the Giver of the holy spirit and the holy spirit is the gift given.

The fulfilment of Joel's prophecy is a departure from how the spirit had been given previously. In previous dispensations, the spirit was given to a few saints and never on all. Now the gift of the spirit was for all saints.

28 And it hath come to pass afterwards, I do pour out My Spirit on all flesh, And prophesied have your sons and your daughters, Your old men do dream dreams, Your young men do see visions. 29 And also on the men-servants, and on the maid-servants, In those days I do pour out My Spirit.
Joel 2:28 – 29 (YLT)

Robert Young's Literal Translation transports us into the world of the ancient Jewish authors by helping us see this prophecy the way that Joel is likely to have given it.

It is as though Joel sees himself as alive in the time of the fulfilment of the prophecy.

Observe that God said, "I will pour out".

He did not say, "I will continue to pour out".

The God-side in redemption is done once. God poured out once. Once is the number of redemption.

The tense used for this outpouring says that God's past action of pouring out the spirit has ongoing effects in the saints today. The idea is that after God has poured out, men started receiving from that singular outpouring. We continue to receive many times from God's one-time out-pouring.

The term, "the gifts of the Spirit" can be a confusing term. Ideally, it is more proper to say, "the gift of the spirit"; for the holy spirit is the gift God gives through the Lord Jesus. It is from this spirit that we subsequently receive tongues and other expressions which manifest the spirit. The human spirit's characteristic of speaking in tongues functions like a faculty or endowment within man. Think of an endowment as a form of inheritance. Greek scholars will refer to this type of gift which functions like an endowment as charisma.

7 But the manifestation of the Spirit is given to every man to profit withal.
1 Corinthians 12: 7

This piece of scripture is pivotal in understanding the ministry of the spirit. Paul's use of the past tense assures us that the giving is a finished work of Christ.

God's gift to us is "Christ in us" and in Him, we have already been blessed with all spiritual blessings via the recreation of our spirits. Our rich inheritance in Christ includes the things of the spirit that Paul speaks of here.

Scholars tell us that in Greek grammar, a past action can have a continuing effect in the now. He is affirming that the things that are already done in Christ are continuing to have an effect in and through us today, by the way of the holy spirit, which Christ had given to us in the New Birth.

When He was on the earth there were instances where the Lord Jesus initiated contact with people and spoke those words which the Father had given to Him and these words brought forth supernatural results as people acted on them (see Luke 17:14).The words of the Father came to those people by the things that Jesus said unto them. Jesus' words registered upon their minds through their physical ears and their actions released the energising of God which were hiding in Jesus' words. This was how Jesus gifted the people with supernatural manifestations.

The Lord Jesus is alive today and He speaks the words of the Father through us by the gift of spirit in us. Although He spoke to those that He ministered to in a mouth-to-ear manner, because we are in Him, He does not speak to us mouth to ear. We know what He is saying by revelation and we speak them forth. What we speak then requires actions on our part or additionally on the part of those that we speak to. As these actions follow from the revelation, the result is that we gift the people with supernatural results. The words of the Father, which the Lord Jesus gives to us are given through the recreated spirit. Our recreated spirit then gives these things to our minds to say to people.

We receive from our spirits and then minister these things to people. We are gifting them with the supernatural delivering power of the Father.

The ability to manifest the spirit is given to us in Christ. How much of the spirit we manifest is up to us. We can express the gift or shy away from the use of it. We would not be good stewards if we are waiting for God to express the gift that He is waiting on us to manifest for His glory.

5

THE GIFT IS GIVEN

33 Therefore being by the right hand of God exalted, and having received of the Father the promise of the Holy Ghost, he hath shed forth this, which ye now see and hear.
Acts 2: 33

It was not until Jesus had ascended into heaven a few days before Pentecost that God glorified Him in the invisible dimension.

On the day of Pentecost, the first act of the Lord Jesus as a glorified one was to give His gift of holy spirit to be received by all that believed on His name. The Lord Jesus has supplied the language we call tongues through that gift of holy spirit. The human spirit does not create the language called tongues. The Lord Jesus is the life-giving Spirit that gives utterance within the spirit of the saint. The spirit of the saint then gives this utterance to be spoken out as tongues by the will of the saint. God never speaks in tongues. Speaking in tongues is not the gift that the Lord Jesus gave to humanity. Speaking in tongues is done in the visible dimension and it is a physical sign of the gift. The gift is the promised spirit, given as the New Birth.

Saints speak in tongues as a way of manifesting the ability of God now resident in their human spirits. Speaking in tongues shows or announces to those around the saint that the believing one is in communion with Jesus, the life-giving Spirit.

The spirit, just like the breath and wind cannot be seen, but its effect can be seen. We can see the manifestation of the invisible spirit. The Lord did not give the manifestations, He gave His spirit as the gift. The nine ways of manifesting the gift of the spirit were the direct effects of Jesus' first act of giving His spirit.

We can understand this fact that the spirit, though invisible, can be discerned by manifestation by observing Elisha after Elijah had been removed from public ministry:

14 And he took the mantle of Elijah that fell from him, and smote the waters,
and said, Where is the LORD God of Elijah? and when he also had smitten
the waters, they parted hither and thither: and Elisha went over. 15 And when
the sons of the prophets which were to view at Jericho saw him, they said, The spirit of Elijah doth rest on Elisha. And they came to meet him, and bowed themselves to the ground before him.

2 Kings 2: 14 - 15

The sons of the prophets said, "The spirit of Elijah doth rest on Elisha." The bible does not say or imply that the sons of the prophets had seen a vision in order to know that the spirit of Elijah rested on Elisha. How could the sons of the prophets tell that the spirit of Elijah rested on Elisha? Although, the spirit was invisible like the wind or breath, the sons of the prophets could tell that the spirit of Elijah rested on Elisha because they saw Elisha manifest that invisible spirit when he used the mantle of Elijah to smite the waters and work a miracle. In other words, although the spirit is invisible, the spirit can be manifested by the one that the spirit is upon.

In the same way, on the day of Pentecost, after permanently receiving the gift of holy spirit without measure from the Lord Jesus, Peter and company operated God's gift of holy spirit and it resulted in those visible manifestations of the spirit which were seen at Pentecost. Those around them should have been able to say that the spirit of the Lord was upon Peter, John and company. We use the manifestation of the spirit to make the spirit known in blessing and power. We often try to divorce the fruit of the spirit from the manifestation of the spirit when both are expressions of the one spirit, which is the gift of God. Prophecy, tongues and interpretation of tongues are not the gift, they are the manifestation of the gift. The gift is the spirit that God gives.

This is the record that we have of Stephen:

8. And Stephen, full of faith and power, did great wonders and miracles among the people.
Acts 6: 8

The word translated power, which is dunamis, refers to an inherent ability which is able to accomplish any task. Faith is a firm confidence, a firm persuasion, a conviction based upon that which we have heard from God through His gift of spirit or from His written Word. Stephen's ability to do great wonders and miracles among the people is tied to the fact that he was full of faith and tremendous power.

In other words, after Stephen received eternal life, over time, he developed into a man that was fully persuaded of the Gospel of Christ that had been preached to him. Stephen's gospel-based persuasion caused him to excel in the reality of the holy spirit within him. God's Word assured Stephen that he was the possessor of God's gift of an intangible holy spirit, although the report of the senses would have said otherwise. As a man of faith, he prioritised the report of God's Word over that of the senses. Receiving the report of God's Word stirred boldness in Stephen to manifest the inherent ability of the spirit.

We can learn some lessons about the manifestation of the spirit from the first outpouring at Pentecost:

4 And they were all filled with the Holy Ghost, and began to speak with other tongues, as the Spirit gave them utterance.
Acts 2: 4

Peter's explanation was that after the Lord Jesus had received the promised spirit from the Father, the first act of the Lord Jesus as a glorified one was to give His gift of holy spirit to be received by all that believed on His name. Therefore, when we see the term "the Holy Ghost" we must realise that this refers to the gift given and not the Giver. The Giver is the Lord (see Acts 2:33). The capitals blind us to the fact that the gift is in view. The correct text is "they were all filled with holy ghost". This means that they all received the gift of the holy spirit, which refers to the new nature sealed into the reborn human spirit. That is the reception of Eternal Life.

The Pentecostal promise from Peter to the crowd was, "ye shall receive the gift of the Holy Ghost" (see Acts 2: 38).

Peter is not speaking of the Holy Ghost as Giver but as the gift given by the Lord Jesus. Thus, it is the dorea (or free gift) of the holy ghost that was the promise of God (see Acts 2:39). This was the gift that Peter and company had received earlier and now the crowd could receive by believing the Gospel. The gift that the Lord poured out at Pentecost was the free gift of the holy spirit. The crowd did not see the Lord pour out that gift since the spirit is intangible and invisible. However, they saw tongues in manifestation. The implication is that after the exaltation of the Lord Jesus, the free gift of holy spirit carried with it the ability to manifest tongues and interpretation of tongues.

This was why as soon as the disciples received the free gift of the spirit, they could manifest tongues by speaking in tongues as the Spirit gave them utterance. That Spirit giving utterance is the Lord Jesus who by His resurrection is the life-giving Spirit (see 1 Corinthians 15:45 and 2 Corinthians 3:17).

Whereas when observed from the senses, it appears that tongues is given by God in addition to and as a separate act from the New Birth. The saint does not possess tongues as a separate reality from the gift of the reborn spirit. When man receives a recreated spirit from the Lord Jesus, one characteristic ability of that spirit is speaking in tongues. A man just as readily speaks in tongues in the New Testament as the saints prophesied when the spirit came upon them in the Old. In fact, it is easier in the New since the holy spirit is the nature of the believer. The holy spirit therefore confers on the believer the ability to speak in tongues and through this, the other manifestations of the same spirit.

Can anyone forbid water?

15 And as I began to speak, the Holy Ghost fell on them, as on us at the beginning. 16 Then remembered I the word of the Lord, how that he said, John indeed baptized with water; but ye shall be baptized with the Holy Ghost. 17 Forasmuch then as God gave them the like gift as he did unto us, who believed on the Lord Jesus Christ; what was I, that I could withstand God?
Acts 11: 15 - 17

Peter finally understood elements of the teaching that Jesus had given in the forty days before He ascended to Heaven. He understood Cornelius' speaking in tongues to be the fulfilment of Jesus' teaching "John indeed baptized with water; but ye shall be baptized with the Holy Ghost". While the Jews were in shock in Cornelius' house, Peter began to recall the teachings of the Lord. Therefore, when Jesus spoke about baptism with the Holy Ghost that baptism could be manifested by speaking in tongues.

According to historians, it was about ten years after Pentecost before the first Gentiles were accepted into the Church. Interestingly, the thing that convinced Peter and company that Gentiles could be Christians was that the gentiles manifested speaking in tongues. Peter and the other Jews saw the Gentiles as dogs who had no covenant with God. Peter's astonishment when Cornelius manifested the spirit by speaking in tongues would be equivalent to the confusion you'd experience if your pet bull-dog breaks up the Church service by speaking in tongues today! That manifestation was the proof that Peter and his crew accepted as witness that Cornelius and his family were born again (see Acts 10:44-47).

Once it was obvious that Cornelius had received the same gift that Peter had received at Pentecost, Peter said, "Can any man forbid water, that these should not be baptized, which have received the Holy Ghost as well as we? (See Acts 10: 47).

What do you think happened next?

Most people would conclude that Cornelius and his household were baptised in water afterwards.

I don't think so.

Why don't I think so?

Well, this is what Peter said:

15 And as I began to speak, the Holy Ghost fell on them, as on us at the beginning. 16 Then remembered I the word of the Lord, how that he said, John indeed baptized with water; but ye shall be baptized with the Holy Ghost. 17 Forasmuch then as God gave them the like gift as he did unto us, who believed on the Lord Jesus Christ; what was I, that I could withstand God?
Acts 11: 15 - 17

Peter said that as Cornelius and his household spoke in tongues he remembered Jesus' teaching "John indeed baptized with water; but ye shall be baptized with the Holy Ghost."

Peter could see that Cornelius already had the greater baptism that Jesus had prophesied and taught about for forty days. This was greater than the water baptism of John.

So, when Peter said, "Can any man forbid water, that these should not be baptized, which have received the Holy Ghost as well as we?"

Peter would have said, "I do".

Cornelius did not only have the gift of holy spirit, he had gone one step further by manifesting that gift just as Peter and company had done at Pentecost. This agrees with the Day of Pentecost that once a man is born again, he has the capacity to manifest the spirit. Ministering this spirit, which is God's gift to us at the New Birth, is at the core of the New Testament. Once we have the gift, it is up to us to minister from that gift by manifesting the spirit. God has given the gift and now His gift to us becomes the origin of various manifestations. We are not waiting for another – we are acting by faith and recognising the divine deposit within.

In natural man, we readily observe the possession of the faculty of speech from birth. We don't receive the power of language asides from our humanity. That power of speech is latent. It is a characteristic of our being human. It is inherent in our humanity. Although we are in possession of the power of speech, we do not all manifest that ability at the same time. Every one speaks in his or her own time. It is the same with manifestation of the spirit. God gave us His spirit in order that we might ably minister that spirit.

17 And these signs shall follow them that believe; In my name shall they cast out devils; they shall speak with new tongues;
Mark 16: 17

Although the disciples of Jesus casted out devils before His death and resurrection, they never spoke in new tongues until after He gave them the gift of holy spirit in the New Birth. Observe that the Lord Jesus did not say that God gives new tongues as a sign to the believer. Instead, He wants us to see that new tongues are a sign manifested by the believer who has the gift of a new spirit. Through this manifestation, the saint is demonstrating that he already possesses a new spirit. Speaking in new tongues is a sign from the new spirit in the believer.

The Lord Jesus is making an important point here. He is presenting tongues as one of the identifying characteristic of those who have believed on the name of Jesus. It is almost as though the new tongues describe the native language of those born again in the Church age. The ability of tongues is like our tribal language. You would expect a man to speak in tongues as long as he is saved. Since salvation in the Church age is permanent, the ability to speak in new tongues which proceeds as a manifestation from the new spirit would also be permanent. This manifestation cannot be lost for the gift of the spirit is permanent. This ability to speak in tongues is so permanent that Paul told the naughty, unruly, divisive and carnal saints in Corinth, "I would that ye all spake with tongues" (see 1 Corinthians 14:5). He could say so because he teaches that tongues is a manifestation of the spirit. Its expression is up to the saint.

Is God the one speaking in new tongues?

14 For if I pray in an unknown tongue, my spirit prayeth, but my understanding is unfruitful.
1 Corinthians 14: 14

The bible clearly shows that God is a speaking God. However, there is nothing in all of God's Word that states that God speaks in tongues. Paul teaches plainly that it is the spirit of the saint that speaks in tongues. Speaking in tongues is my human spirit speaking. Tongues is a characteristic or proof produced by the spirit of truth. It is the supply of comfort from the born-again spirit, which is the comforter that Jesus had promised.

The two Adams

The bible summarises the history of man in two Adams. Each Adam represents the beginning of something. The first Adam never quite lived up to the lofty ideals that God had in mind for man. In the first Adam, death passed upon all men in that he made an appointment of death for all men. Each man then keeps that appointment by their individual disobedience of unbelief which produces death in them. Even then, the bible shows us that until the confusion of languages, which Moses recorded in Genesis, all the people spoke the language ushered in by the first Adam (see Genesis 11:1).

In his writings, Paul refers to the Lord Jesus Christ as the last Adam (see 1 Corinthians 15:45). This last Adam gives the spirit as life and righteousness through faith in the Gospel. This last Adam also gives to His own people a language. All that are in the last Adam manifest the new language by faith.

The height of priesthood in the first Adam was the Levitical priesthood under the Law. That priesthood was a brotherhood with common genetics and a common language. In much the same way that all of Levi were one tribe speaking one language, all that are of Christ demonstrate the attributes of the new nation in Christ. In that nation, we are one tribe of holy and royal priests (see 1 Peter 2:9).

14 For if I pray in an unknown tongue, my spirit prayeth, but my understanding is unfruitful. 15 What is it then? I will pray with the spirit, and I will pray with the understanding also: I will sing with the spirit, and I will sing with the understanding also.
1 Corinthians 14: 14 - 15

Talking is a characteristic of all spirits. However, talking in tongues is uniquely of the recreated spirit which man receives from the Lord Jesus. That same spirit of truth that speaks in tongues also prays in tongues and can sing in tongues. Thus, according to Paul, we are to see tongues as an activity that the spirit of the saint expresses in diversities.

The ability to speak in tongues is of the recreated spirit. It is a characteristic of that spirit, even the comforter, which we have received of God. When a man is given scriptural knowledge about the possibility of tongues that information helps the mind receive the expression of tongues. Perhaps the most mind-boggling fact is that even those Christians who teach that tongues have passed away have the faculty for tongues within them; for Christ has given to all saints, the same gift of holy spirit in the new creation through the New Birth. Whether expressed or not the tongues is there and resident within the spirit of the born again one.

Tongues as a proof of more

The Lord gives the singular gift of a new spirit and within that spirit various abilities. The Lord Jesus gives utterance to the spirit, the spirit then gives that utterance to the human will and the saint then speaks it out. This shows that the real gist of Peter's sermon at Pentecost is that tongues is proof that the spirit which the Lord Jesus has given to His own is also a giving spirit (see Acts 2:32-33).

In that sense, tongues is a parable that says that all the blessings of the spirit are already present and ready to be manifested. The presence of tongues from the spirit of man says that utterance, revelation and power are resident in the same spirit. God is responsible for giving us the spirit. We are responsible for gaining understanding and insight from God's Word about all that is hidden within that spirit. It is supplied abundantly in the Epistles.

Acknowledging what is rightful yours

1 And I, brethren, could not speak unto you as unto spiritual, but as unto carnal, even as unto babes in Christ.
1 Corinthians 3: 1

Paul is addressing the same saints that he acknowledged as not coming behind in any gift (see 1 Corinthians 1:4-7). They did not come behind in any gift because in spite of their carnality and worldliness, they had received the gift of the spirit which the Lord gave in the New Birth. Although, they did not come behind in any gift, he says, "You are babes". The sense of what he is saying is, "You are operating these gifts as babes".

A babe, whether spiritual or natural, is not ready to acknowledge what is already rightfully his or hers. In the natural, babies have realities that they cannot explain to others. Although they came behind in no gift, they had operated in the things of the spirit as babes. These Corinthians had not acknowledged or accepted that their spirits operated in love.

Paul said this affected the way that he fed them with spiritual food. This means that he taught them as though they were carnal, natural men even though they were spiritual men in Christ.

Paul was saying, "I know who you are. You are in the spirit. However, considering who you are, there is a way I should have addressed you and communicated to you but what you haven't acknowledged about yourself is dictating how I speak to you. You are really of Christ and complete in Him but I have addressed you as though I can only get to you from the outer man. Therefore, I have been limited to parabolic speech when I should have used great plainness of speech".

37 If any man think himself to be a prophet, or spiritual, let him acknowledge that the things that I write unto you are the commandments of the Lord.
1 Corinthians 14: 37

Paul ended up addressing these Corinthians as spiritual. That is what he was doing with his excellent teaching on spirituals. His instructions to the Corinthians mirror his instruction to Timothy about flowing in the spirit.

6 Wherefore I put thee in remembrance that thou stir up the gift of God, which is in thee by the putting on of my hands. 7 For God hath not given us the spirit of fear; but of power, and of love, and of a sound mind.
2 Timothy 1: 6 - 7

Paul's instruction to Timothy was spoken to a man that had a new spirit. You observe that in some respects, Timothy was living in timidity and fear. Paul did not tell Timothy to go to God and beg for new gifts. Instead, he reminded Timothy that the spirit that he had already received from God at the New Birth was not a spirit of fear. The born-again spirit does not reason like, "what if I say the wrong thing". The recreated spirit does not assume that we will be wrong. If you goofed just get up and go for it again.

14 Neglect not the gift that is in thee, which was given thee by prophecy, with the laying on of the hands of the presbytery. 15 Meditate upon these things; give thyself wholly to them; that thy profiting may appear to all.
1 Timothy 4: 14 - 15

Paul told Timothy to remember to meditate upon what Timothy had received, stay stirred up and most importantly not to neglect it. The spirit must be believed in order for us to manifest and demonstrate it.

Paul had this to say to the Corinthians:

Now concerning spiritual gifts, brethren, I would not have you ignorant. 2 Ye know that ye were Gentiles, carried away unto these dumb idols, even as ye were led. 3 Wherefore I give you to understand, that no man speaking by the Spirit of God calleth Jesus accursed: and that no man can say that Jesus is the Lord, but by the Holy Ghost.
1 Corinthians 12:1 - 3

To whom did Paul write these words?

He was writing to the Corinthian Church that he had acknowledged did not come behind in any gift.

So, Paul told a Church already enriched in spiritual instruction, "I would not have you ignorant". They were not unfamiliar with the supernatural but what they lacked prompted Paul to classify them as ignorant (or unlearned as he would later call them).

What did he mean by "I would not have you ignorant"?

The ignorance does not necessarily mean that the people he was speaking to were in the dark about the things of the spirit. He meant that he does not want them to lack the clear thinking and understanding that beautifies our administration of spiritual flow. We can know his meaning by what he gave to them to combat their ignorance. Paul said, "I give you to understand".

Paul was saying that saints should understand the things of the spirit and not just experience them. It is a New Testament requirement for the saint to be a person of understanding.

Paul was not merely trying to get them more knowledgeable. He wanted them to understand spirituals by giving them insight into the full orbit of spiritual flow. This is what Paul covered under the concepts of operation (verse 6), administration (verse 5), and the gifts (verse 4).

The Corinthian letter shows that those who had been enriched in knowledge, additionally need understanding so that they might become decent and orderly in spiritual flow. There are further things to be taught to those who have already started out on the journey of manifesting the spirit. These births understanding, which increases effectiveness. The implication is that our effectiveness in spiritual flow improves with understanding. When you intelligently act on what the spirit gives you, you are perpetuating the ministries of the spirit. You become better with prayer, practice and further study in that order.

What we find is that every time Paul wrote about utterance, whether to Timothy or the Corinthians, he wrote to people who already spoke in tongues. This means that utterance is experiential. Most of what he wrote was with the intent of fine-tuning the operations of those who already spoke in tongues. This shows that instructions about utterance work best for practitioners. You will not become proficient in utterance merely by reading this book. However, the book will make the greatest impact, if you are already given to speaking in tongues. The fellow who is sitting on the fence on these matters will not benefit much from the force of Paul's instructions. He was not writing to seminarians who wanted to trump each other's arguments in cyberspace. He was writing to practitioners. He was looking to fine tune their practice so they could be more effective.

Quench not the spirit

19 Quench not the Spirit. 20 Despise not prophesyings. 21 Prove all things; hold fast that which is good.
1 Thessalonians 5: 19 - 21

Some take Paul's instruction to mean that when people prophesy to us or minister to us by the spirit, we should take what we find agreeable in their ministration and throw away the others that don't jive with the cumulative slant of God's dealings with us. There is some wisdom in that. However, the intent of Paul was not to show that there is that which is "not good" in the flow of the spirit.

That word "prove" means to make invisible things visible. You can only prove that which you haven't quenched. It is a sober fact that we have the power to quench the spirit.

You don't fall into the danger of quenching God. You face the grave danger of quenching the spirit, which is God's gift to you in Christ. That spirit refers to the human spirit. You can dampen the fire of the human spirit or you can let it become a raging inferno.

The major reason why people quench the spirit is because they are ignorant about the ways of the spirit; therefore, they do not desire or covet the things that they should. Another reason is because of unbelief. Many saints perceive the promptings but they doubt it; they receive doubt from their minds rather than faith from the spirit through the Word. Then there are people that are disobedient – they will not respond to the spirit although they know better.

If you hold back from experimenting with those urges and impressions that the spirit gives, you dampen the flames of the spirit. Your ignorance, indecision, unbelief and doubt quench the spirit from being manifested. You can train your will and mind on God's Word, so that you overcome that tendency to quench the spirit.

The reason for not quenching the spirit is so that we may hold fast the things that are already true in the spirit. That is, of the things that are not quenched, we will be able to hold fast to some things. Concerning utterance or the vocal expressions of the spirit, the effect that we are to hold on to is edification. The apostle has said that utterance as tongues or prophecy brings edification. He doesn't just want you to know that the way a theologian knows a fact; he wants you to prove it. You are to prove that edification is contained within utterance. You can only do so by speaking in tongues and experimenting with speaking in tongues until you understand how you lay hold of maximum edification. As saints, we are to explore the different uses of the things of the spirit. When you do that, you are laying hold on that which is good about tongues, which is edification.

Although the Word declares that when you speak in tongues you will be edified, you cannot hold on to the edification when you have not proven the tongues. Tongues is part of the all things that you prove. This proving will make the invisible edification effectual.

You are to hold on to the edification. Speaking in tongues represents fanning the flame or stoking the fire. You can only hold fast that which you have fanned to flame.

There are spiritual things that are true that you can only benefit from by persevering in holding fast to continual practice. The tendency is to ignore these things because they are not immediately visible to us. He is giving us vital information on how to make it visible. There is much good to be harvested from spiritual flow but it requires proving by not quenching the spirit. The Word gives you the responsibility of proving by locating the benefit and holding on to it.

It is up to us to quench the spirit or to prove the things of the spirit. Paul is saying, "Quench not the gift of the holy spirit which you have received from the Lord but prove that its manifestation brings edification to your world".

6

SPIRITUAL SENSES

Now concerning spiritual gifts, brethren, I would not have you ignorant. 2 Ye know that ye were Gentiles, carried away unto these dumb idols, even as ye were led. 3 Wherefore I give you to understand, that no man speaking by the Spirit of God calleth Jesus accursed: and that no man can say that Jesus is the Lord, but by the Holy Ghost.
1 Corinthians 12:1 - 3

The word "gifts" is italicised in the KJV because the translators want us to know there is no such word in the verse. This was added by them. The Greek word which is translated "spiritual" is 'pneumatikos' and it means "that which pertains to the spirit". It describes the characteristics by which Christ's gift, the holy spirit, shows its presence. That spirit is the spirit of man.

Paul provides thought provoking insight concerning some attributes of the spiritual faculty in man.

…concerning spirituals (v1), …no man speaking by the Spirit of God (v3), …but the same spirit (v4), …manifestation of the spirit (v7), …given by the spirit (v8), …by the same spirit (v9), …by the same spirit (v9), …that one and the self same Spirit (v11), …by one spirit (v13), …drink into one spirit (v13).

All the above are various references to the singular gift of the spirit which Christ gives to give the status of sonship, righteousness, holiness and power in those that believe.

The chapter teaches that the spirit would be manifested by the saints seeing, hearing and speaking.

When we examine these manifestations, we find that although the characteristic of seeing, hearing and speaking is the same in the spirit of all saints, the level of knowledge conveyed from the spirit to the mind through various spiritual experiences varies with spiritual maturity; this is measured by the understanding of those who have the experience. Although the illustration below is not a manifestation of the spirit, it demonstrates the fact our minds do not equally register what our spiritual faculties pick up even when we have been exposed to the same spiritual inputs:

The Gospel is the power of God

Although all saints have the same gift of holy spirit, we do not all benefit equally from the things that the spirit gives to our minds because the intensity to which we have exposed our minds to the written Word is not the same for all. Tradition and unbelief in the mind blunts the ability to absorb insight from the spirit.

Consider Paul's Damascus experience:

Here is Paul's testimony before King Agrippa, a non-Jew:

*13 At midday, O king, I saw in the way a light from heaven, above the
brightness of the sun, shining round about me and them which journeyed with
me. 14 And when we were all fallen to the earth, I heard a voice speaking unto
me, and saying in the Hebrew tongue, Saul, Saul, why persecutest thou me? it is
hard for thee to kick against the pricks. 15 And I said, Who art thou, Lord?
And he said, I am Jesus whom thou persecutest. 16 But rise, and stand upon thy
feet: for I have appeared unto thee for this purpose, to make thee a minister and*

a witness both of these things which thou hast seen, and of those things in the which I will appear unto thee; 17 Delivering thee from the people, and from the Gentiles, unto whom now I send thee, 18 To open their eyes, and to turn them from darkness to light, and from the power of Satan unto God, that they may receive forgiveness of sins, and inheritance among them which are sanctified by faith that is in me. 19 Whereupon, O king Agrippa, I was not disobedient unto the heavenly vision:

Acts 26:13 - 19

Since Paul told Agrippa, "O king Agrippa, I was not disobedient unto the heavenly vision", we know that this is a vision. As a minister, Paul discussed spiritual things with King Agrippa. He did not discuss politics. Agrippa needs to hear the Gospel too. The New Testament minister is not sent to kings or presidents to discuss politics.

Although, Paul heard the voice identify Himself as Jesus, he did not see the Lord in person-form. The sequence is that Paul saw the light, after which he fell to the ground and then he heard the voice. It was from within this envelope of light that the voice that Paul heard came from. The voice was contained within the light.

A voice in the Hebrew tongue

What are we to make of Saul's statement, "I heard a voice speaking unto me, and saying in the Hebrew tongue"?

The fact that Paul heard the voice in the Hebrew tongue does not mean that God speaks Hebrew per se, it means that Hebrew was the language that Paul's mind used to capture his understanding of what was happening. The communication registered upon Paul's mind in Hebrew. The Hebrew is from the perspective of the hearer. If Paul was English-speaking, it would have appeared to him that God spoke to him in the English tongue. God does not communicate through our biological senses but through our spiritual senses. He does this via revelation. Divine revelation is hearing and seeing through the inward senses of the human spirit. It is the spiritual equivalent of hearing and seeing biologically. Divine revelation flows from God's Spirit to our spirit primarily through thoughts and impressions. Although, revelation imparts insight, it is not directly through the knowledge of any human language itself; rather, the meaning and thoughts of God are communicated directly and instantaneously.

God does not speak in human language even though we seem to hear God in the language that we are conversant with in our natural minds. When you hear God speak to you in your vernacular, it is not that He actually verbalised your vernacular. He communicates (spiritually) to your spirit man at a depth too high for the human language to transmit. Your human spirit then steps this down for the benefit of your intellect in your everyday vernacular. Therefore, at the point that it registers on your soul, you are convinced in your mind that God spoke your vernacular.

When saints appear to hear God speak to them in a human language, what is happening is that they are recognising the moment that their mind understands what their spirit already knows. At that point, saints become conscious of the gift of holy spirit conveying to their minds, the revelation which their spirits had grasped without earthly language. Divine revelation is an impartation of experience and knowledge. The flow of spiritual facts is like data exchange between two mobile phones. However, divine revelation is more than a flow of facts. Divine revelation transfers full experiences and sensations.

Paul never said that his travel companions understood what was going on. Although they experienced the supernatural, they were none the clearer for it. Paul's advantage was not in seeing the light but in his understanding what he saw. He understood the spiritual things that his companions were ignorant of. He concentrated more on what he heard than on what he saw. Paul never really said that he directly saw the Lord on the road to Damascus. He clearly heard and understood the voice of the Lord. Paul was the only one conversing with the voice because he was the only one that could distinguish what the voice was saying unto him.

Luke gives a fascinating account of the same vision:

3 And as he journeyed, he came near Damascus: and suddenly there shined round about him a light from heaven: 4 And he fell to the earth, and heard a voice saying unto him, Saul, Saul, why persecutest thou me? 5 And he said, Who art thou, Lord? And the Lord said, I am Jesus whom thou persecutest: it is hard for thee to kick against the pricks. 6 And he trembling and astonished said, Lord, what wilt thou have me to do? And the Lord said unto him, Arise, and go into the city, and it shall be told thee what thou must do. 7 And the men which journeyed with him stood speechless, hearing a voice, but seeing no man. 8 And Saul arose from the earth; and when his eyes were opened, he saw no man: but they led him by the hand, and brought him into Damascus.

Acts 9:3 - 8

Luke's account shows that Saul had his physical eyes closed all through this vision; for It was at the end of the vision that Saul opened his eyes and discovered that he could not see. Therefore, the light that Saul saw was not in an open vision. It was a mental picture. However, since we are not told that the natural eyes of his travel companions were closed, it is likely that they all had an open vision. His companions could see both the spiritual light and their environment. Paul's companions did not also see the Lord.

Paul did not hear by seeing. He used his spiritual ears to hear and his spiritual eyes to see. The faculties for spiritual sound as well as spiritual vision were engaged in Paul, for he saw the light and heard the voice that spoke. Paul picked up more information from what he heard in this vision than what he saw. This is like television with amplified sound.

When Paul recounted this very vision before fellow Jews, he emphasised a different aspect.

6 And it came to pass, that, as I made my journey, and was come nigh unto Damascus about noon, suddenly there shone from heaven a great light round about me. 7 And I fell unto the ground, and heard a voice saying unto me, Saul, Saul, why persecutest thou me? 8 And I answered, Who art thou, Lord? And he said unto me, I am Jesus of Nazareth, whom thou persecutest. 9 And they that were with me saw indeed the light, and were afraid; but they heard not the voice of him that spake to me. 10 And I said, What shall I do, LORD? And the Lord said unto me, Arise, and go into Damascus; and there it shall be told thee of all things which are appointed for thee to do. 11 And when I could not see for the glory of that light, being led by the hand of them that were with me, I came into Damascus. 12 And one Ananias, a devout man according to the law, having a good report of all the Jews which dwelt there, 13 Came unto me, and stood, and said unto me, Brother Saul, receive thy sight. And the same hour I looked up upon him. 14 And he said, The God of our fathers hath chosen thee, that thou shouldest know his will, and see that Just One, and shouldest hear the voice of his mouth.

Acts 22:6 - 14

Paul was speaking to fellow Jews who were accustomed to the supernatural; therefore, he added greater detail when telling the Jews about his vision.

What do we make of that expression, "And they that were with me saw indeed the light, and were afraid; but they heard not the voice of him that spake to me"?

Rather than engage in a conversation with the voice speaking within the light like Saul did, those traveling with Saul were overcome with fear. Their own fear prevented them from comprehending the spiritual sounds. This shows that fear registers as noise upon the heart of man. It dulls the spiritual senses and distorts our spiritual understanding by reducing the rate at which the heart absorbs spiritual facts. The very sounds that had registered upon Saul's mind in the Hebrew tongue were unintelligent to his companions. That sound was not different things to different people, it's just that Saul's mind was free from fear where theirs wasn't. Saul and his companions heard a voice but only Saul understood it. The benefit is neither in seeing the light nor in hearing the sound but in a heart devoid of fear.

Prioritising the written Word

It is a spiritual fact that two people can be exposed to the same spiritual experience but come out with completely different interpretations of their spiritual experiences. Consider Elisha and his assistant:

15 And when the servant of the man of God was risen early, and gone forth,
behold, an host compassed the city both with horses and chariots. And his servant
said unto him, Alas, my master! how shall we do? 16 And he answered, Fear
not: for they that be with us are more than they that be with them. 17 And
Elisha prayed, and said, Lord, I pray thee, open his eyes, that he may see.
And the Lord opened the eyes of the young man; and he saw: and, behold, the
mountain was full of horses and chariots of fire round about Elisha.
2 Kings 16:15 - 17

Elisha's assistant was highly developed in the spirit of fear and gave voice to it. His Word content was zero. He was that kind of fellow who assumed that the supernatural was beyond the sphere of his comprehension.

When Elisha said, "they that be with us are more than they that be with them", he was operating in faith and using the written Word to comfort his assistant. His assistant wouldn't accept the testimony of the written Word, therefore, he couldn't receive the comfort of scriptures from Elisha. Elisha's declaration contained more spiritual light than the vision that his disciple would end up seeing. We are not told that Elisha saw a vision in this instance. He did not need one. He was already operating on the revelation knowledge that he had received from the written Word.

Since Elisha's servant wouldn't receive comfort from scriptures, Elisha asked God to give his assistant a vision and the assistant saw a vision as a result of Elisha's prayer. This shows that visions are not completely up to God! Others can see visions in response to our supplication. We have to learn this.

In the vision, the assistant couldn't see the horses and chariots of fire round about himself. Why would the Lord give the assistant a vision of horses and chariots surrounding Elisha when it was the assistant that was in need of that vision?

The fact that Elisha's assistant did not see himself surrounded helps us see that it was his ignorance that veiled him from seeing correctly. He could not see himself as the protected one of the Lord. His own fear had left him defenceless. The vision replayed to him where his fear and unbelief had located him. He believed that Elisha was protected while he was open to attack. That servant was not cooperating with the assistance that God had deployed to protect him. The human mind plays a large role in the imagery that we see in visions. This assistant was seeing the effects of his fear in a visual form.

The information that Elisha's assistant harvested through that vision reflected the assistant's level of understanding. A man who prioritises the written Word would receive more light through the same vision.

A vision is not as important as the actions that arise from it or the conclusions that we draw from it. The conclusions we draw after seeing a vision say nothing about the vision, they say something about us. The interpretation you give a vision will confirm to you whether you are a man of understanding who is full of the Word or not.

The assistant saw horses and chariots of fire in his vision. The Word does not tell us that the assistant understood anything as a result. The fact that a person sees a vision does not mean he gets its meaning. The point is that visions of themselves do not confer upon the one that saw the vision, any spirituality or spiritual depth. The content of the vision might actually indicate that you have not been paying attention to the written Word! God wasn't trying to get Elisha's assistant into horse trading or racing. It is much easier to arrive at the wrong conclusions if one makes the mistake of prioritizing visions above the written Word. Although the assistant clearly saw horses and chariots of fire, that vision had nothing to do with horse trading strategies or secrets of investing into the chariot business. The meaning had nothing to do with literal horses. Without being established in the Word that assistant would arrive at the wrong conclusions from a God-given vision. It seems that the less light that we have in God's Word in an area, the more intensely symbolic our visions will be in that area.

His assistant's vision was the visual representation of what Elisha had tried to tell his assistant much earlier when he said, "they that be with us are more than they that be with them". If the assistant had believed Elisha's report, in his vision he would have seen that horses and chariots of fire surrounded both himself and Elisha and not just Elisha. In that sense, his vision was a warning for him to abandon unbelief. Since the vision is not doctrinal, it will not teach him how to abandon unbelief.

17 And Elisha prayed, and said, Lord, I pray thee, open his eyes, that he may see. And the Lord opened the eyes of the young man; and he saw: and, behold, the mountain was full of horses and chariots of fire round about Elisha.
2 Kings 16:17

When Elisha asked, "Lord, I pray thee, open his eyes that he may see", He was referring to God opening the man's spiritual eyes. The fact is that one could see the right things in a vision and still attach wrong interpretations to them due to not having a clear understanding of God's Word. The level of knowledge communicated through the Word is far more than that which is available directly through a vision only.

When Elisha asked, "Lord, I pray thee, open his eyes, that he may see", the vision granted to the assistant did not bring the angels. Those angels had been there all along. The opening of the eyes of Elisha's assistant helped him receive input from his spiritual sense of vision. His seeing helped him interact with the spiritual realities that had always been around him.

Spiritual senses

Consider Peter's encounter in his prison cell.

7 And, behold, the angel of the Lord came upon him, and a light shined in the prison: and he smote Peter on the side, and raised him up, saying, Arise up quickly. And his chains fell off from his hands.
Acts 12:7

In this vision, many of Peter's spiritual faculties were engaged.

The angel that appeared to Peter in prison had come to administer supernatural deliverance to him.

Peter was fast asleep when the light shone in the prison. It was with his spiritual eyes that Peter saw the light of that angel. Although he was still asleep, his spiritual faculties were at work.

The angel initially ministered to Peter by smiting him on the side as he slept. Peter experienced a degree of pressure consistent with being smitten. This did not come across to Peter as a light touch. This hints at a spiritual sense of pressure that was perceptible to Peter in his sleep.

Peter woke up in the physical as a result of this spiritual pressure.

Though he was no longer asleep, the vision, which had started in his sleep, continued into his waking moments. His physical eyes could now see the environment while his spiritual eyes continued to see the spiritual light. This was now an open vision since Peter saw the gates open, saw the chains and even likely heard them fall. In this vision, Peter saw the angel, heard his voice and felt or sensed spiritual pressure. So, Peter exercised the spiritual senses of sight, pressure and sound simultaneously. He interacted with both the spiritual and the physical worlds simultaneously.

It seemed to Peter that the whole experience was mental and not real. Since it was a vision, the soldiers in that cell with him would not have seen that light. Although, had they been awake they might have seen and heard his hand-chains drop.

While this supernatural deliverance was being executed, Peter saw the angel and He heard the angel's voice giving him instructions. Whether Peter understood the instructions given in that open vision or not was not up to the angel. That was up to Peter.

What Peter understood from what he had seen and heard was not imparted by the vision but by his own spiritual development. Another person would have heard only noise. Peter was spiritually developed. This was observable in that not only could he see and hear in this vision, he could correctly interpret the meaning of the voice. It is as we continue to hear the Word, that we are tuning our inner sense of hearing, so that we can hear more accurately into the spiritual dimension.

These various examples point to the fact that there are spiritual senses that receive input from the spirit realm.

9 But as it is written, Eye hath not seen, nor ear heard, neither have entered into the heart of man, the things which God hath prepared for them that love him.
1 Corinthians 2:9

Salvation is what God had prepared for those that love Him.

The spirit man's anatomy has a spiritual characteristic corresponding to each biological sense in our physical body. Just as in the natural, the spiritual eyes will see and the spiritual ear will hear. The difference between the natural senses and the spiritual senses are the source of their inputs. The inputs and sensations of the spiritual senses are from the spirit realm.

You could say that my spiritual neck fills up my physical neck, just as my spiritual tongue and eyes fill up my physical tongue and eyes respectively. My spiritual brain also fills up my natural brain and it is within this spiritual brain that you have that which we sometimes refer to as the mind, will and emotion.

The spiritual eyes and ears are the means of receiving spiritual information into the heart. You don't hear with your spiritual eyes nor do you see with your spiritual ears. The implication of this is that the spiritual mouth also functions like the natural mouth. Therefore, the spiritual mouth will transmit that which the spiritual eyes, ears and other senses have received in the spirit realm.

14 For if I pray in an unknown tongue, my spirit prayeth, but my understanding is unfruitful.
1 Corinthians 14:14

What Paul said here is only true of the born again human spirit which is only found in Christ. Those who are born of God have the ability of a new language built into their spirit man. Tongues is a characteristic of the born-again spirit in man. Only the recreated spirit can speak in tongues. While it is true that the spirit of the one who is not born again communicates, that communication cannot be tongues. Speaking in tongues is a characteristic of the spirit of the born again one. The saint is the one speaking. While one does not have to be a saint to have visions and dreams, speaking in tongues is exclusive to the born-again man.

15 What is it then? I will pray with the spirit, and I will pray with the understanding also: I will sing with the spirit, and I will sing with the understanding also.
1 Corinthians 14: 15

Speaking in tongues is subject to the will of man. We yield our will and vocal chords and use the combination of the two to manifest the gift of holy spirit by speaking in tongues. Speaking in tongues is yielding your physical tongue to your spiritual tongue so you can speak spiritual utterances generated within your spirit. The spirit generates this utterance within your spiritual mind, which resides within your natural mind. The utterances that become tongues are not accessible through the biological ear but through the spiritual ear. Although you can hear other people speak in tongues through your biological ear, you don't hear the human spirit supplying the utterance to you in your biological ear. As you exercise these faculties of your spirit man, you'll come to pick up the spiritual impressions that will become tongues with your spiritual senses. Some people even see the words with their spiritual eye in an inner vision.

4 And they were all filled with the Holy Ghost, and began to speak with other tongues, as the Spirit gave them utterance.
Acts 2: 4

If we read this in the light of the understanding contained within Paul's "I will pray with the spirit, and I will pray with the understanding also", we can see the following:

The Lord Jesus is the Spirit that gives the utterance through His gift of spirit in the saint. The indwelling spirit then gives this utterance to our will. This process involves our will empowering our spiritual mouth to voice out new sounds through our physical mouth. This is how the reborn spirit gives tongues to the outer man to speak out.

2 For he that speaketh in an unknown tongue speaketh not unto men, but unto God: for no man understandeth him; howbeit in the spirit he speaketh mysteries.
1 Corinthians 14:2

When you speak mysteries or religious secrets in tongues, your spiritual mouth through your physical mouth is emptying out the revelation and religious secrets that your spirit already has. Since our spirits are having a divine communion when speaking in tongues, the things spoken in tongues are not secrets to our recreated spirits. Our recreated spirits are having a conversation with God as the audience.

When we speak in tongues, we are expressing through our physical tongue, those secrets, which are already in our spirits. Speaking in tongues is communicating the secrets already possessed in your spirit. Tongues puts into sound form the inner perception and knowings of the recreated spirit.

A man who speaks in tongues is using his spiritual mind, his spiritual tongue, his will and his physical tongue to express what he has already received through his spiritual senses. Therefore, speaking in tongues is not your spiritual senses receiving spiritual secrets. The act of speaking in tongues is not a download into the spirit of man. The spirit of man is preparing a download which will later quiet his mind. It is a means by which the human spirit gives to the other parts of man's constitution. Through speaking in tongues, the human spirit is giving its profit of edification.

7 But the manifestation of the Spirit is given to every man to profit withal.
1 Corinthians 12:7

When we manifest the gift of holy spirit, we give the edification contained within our tongues to other men by causing them to understand what we have spoken in tongues. In public ministry, the only reason for speaking in tongues is so that we might then give the edification contained within it through interpretation. What is true of tongues is true of every other spiritual operation.

7

BEYOND JOHN'S BAPTISM

20 Brethren, be not children in understanding: howbeit in malice be ye children, but in understanding be men.
1 Corinthians 14: 20

It is a distinguishing characteristic of saints who are spiritual babes that they are children in their understanding and in malice they are men.

Paul's statement, "in understanding be men", means that we are to understand the things of that spirit, which we received in the New Birth. The truth of the sufficiency that we received of Christ when we received the gift of a new spirit does not change, it is our grasp of it that changes. The understanding of the things of the spirit is in degrees. We progress from a kindergarten grasp of truth to understanding as men in Christ. The truths we understood in a childish way should become clearer to us as we grow up spiritually. This statement implies that the things of the spirit do not have to be mysterious, for they are unfolded to us in the revelation of Christ. They are to be taught so clearly that those who are taught understand it enough to teach others too. When it comes to utterance, we are to be men.

Laying hold of the spirit

And it came to pass, that, while Apollos was at Corinth, Paul having passed through the upper coasts came to Ephesus: and finding certain disciples, 2 He said unto them, Have ye received the Holy Ghost since ye believed? And they said unto him, We have not so much as heard whether there be any Holy Ghost.
Acts 19:1 - 2

When Paul got to Ephesus, in response to his question to them, the folks at Ephesus famously told him, "We have not so much as heard whether there be a Holy Ghost". This explains why there was no manifestation of the spirit in Ephesus prior to Paul coming there. The people were children in their understanding of Christ's gift of a new spirit.

Paul's question was, "Have ye received the Holy Ghost since ye believed"?

Ghost or spirit in this verse can be small or capitals. If it refers to the Giver, that should be "Ghost" and if it is the gift, it should be ghost. The translators of the KJV have given us an implied interpretation by rendering it as Ghost. The spirit that is received on believing the Gospel is Christ's gift of God's divine nature to man, which is referred to as the promised spirit or the gift of holy spirit. As a paraphrase, Paul is asking if they received a new spirit.

In Paul's letter to the Ephesians, he states this as fact and no longer as a question (see Ephesians 1:13).

Paul could tell that these disciples had not laid hold of the singular gift that Christ gives to those that believe. There was a response he had anticipated in those who believed and this response was conspicuously absent at Ephesus. Paul implied that the manifestation of the spirit was missing in Ephesus. A disciple is not just anyone on the street. Disciples are primarily products of doctrine and practice. Paul could see that these were disciplined followers of an incomplete teaching.

Paul does not ask the Ephesians, "Have you asked God?"

He places the full responsibility on the one who believes. Paul did not first go to them saying that they should come to him in order to get something that was lacking in their lives. He pointed them to what they can "lay hold of" by faith. His question suggests that any time a believing one needed a supply of the spirit, they are to receive because they are already believing ones. The Greek word translated receive in that verse is a word that could also be correctly translated as "to take hold of".

This "taking hold of" is not about reaching out to collect something from God in heaven. It is reaching within and receiving from the indwelling spirit which is the power from on high. Paul is really saying that it is up to the saint to take hold of the deposit that is already present in his or her life. These things are included in the New Birth.

Although much earlier in the book of Acts (see Acts 8), Peter and John had already demonstrated that people could receive the gift of holy ghost into manifestation by the laying on of hands, Paul's question implies that he did not initially see a need to even lay hands on the disciples at Ephesus. The laying on of hands is a way of accelerating saints' recognition of the spirit's presence and power. Paul anticipated that the saints at Ephesus would not need others to have to lay hands on them.

When the fellows at Ephesus responded with, "We have not so much heard whether there be a holy ghost", Paul could see the problem. The problem at Ephesus was that they had not come in contact with anyone who had preached those truths to them so they could hear and believe.

You cannot receive the unknown into manifestation.

Reception is deliberate and you receive to the degree to which you have light. These disciples were diligently following as far as they had light but their light was dim. Ignorance is a sure way to quench the spirit and prevents its manifestation.

If the saint is taught about God's sufficiency present within the indwelling spirit received at the New Birth, that saint is emboldened to receive speaking in tongues as a manifestation of that spirit at any time. Clear instructions help the saints to manifest the spirit in tongues for the first time and every time afterwards. Although, it is scriptural to do so, it is not mandatory to lay hands on the saint in order that the saint might speak in tongues.

4 I thank my God always on your behalf, for the grace of God which is given you by Jesus Christ; 5 That in every thing ye are enriched by him, in all utterance, and in all knowledge;
1 Corinthians 1: 4 – 5

The grace of God is already given in Christ and that grace is all utterance. In Christ, every saint has utterance. There are no born again ones who do not have the inheritance of utterance in Christ Jesus. Utterance is the inheritance of the saint in the name of Jesus. We are to help the saint see that the singular gift is the spirit, which is given in Christ and that all else, including utterance, is conveyed through that gift which has been made available in Christ starting at the New Birth.

All the confusion, drama and gymnastics that tends to accompany trying to get believers to speak in tongues is a measure of how much we do not clearly show the saint that the holy spirit, which is the recreated spirit, is his inheritance in Christ. It is the cobwebs in our thinking, coupled with centuries old tradition and unbelief that hinders the believer from laying hold of the holy spirit when it comes to utterance. God does not give utterance apart from the gift of a new spirit. Once you have a new spirit, you have utterance contained within that gift in Christ.

The saint firmly grasps his inheritance in Christ and puts it to use by speaking in other tongues. Most people do not lay hold of utterance by themselves because they do not know whether there be any holy ghost. They need to be helped. Receiving utterance from the Lord Jesus through the gift of a new spirit by faith is not the only method.

4 Then said Paul, John verily baptized with the baptism of repentance, saying unto the people, that they should believe on him which should come after him, that is, on Christ Jesus. 5 When they heard this, they were baptized in the name

of the Lord Jesus. 6 And when Paul had laid his hands upon them, the Holy Ghost came on them; and they spake with tongues, and prophesied. 7 And all the men were about twelve.
Acts 19:4 - 7

In Ephesus, Paul encountered disciples of John's baptism who did not know that they could receive utterance from the Lord through the indwelling spirit by faith.

Paul was not in a hurry to lay hands on these disciples. He knew that they were helped the best when they know the rich deposits that already belong to them in Christ. It is pneumatology based on Christology. The saint that can be trusted with the supernatural is that one that knows what Christ has done. Saints receive boldness from being grounded in the fact that holy spirit is an inheritance in Christ. They need to know this.

Later in his Epistle to these saints in Ephesians, Paul said the following:

2 Grace be to you, and peace, from God our Father, and from the Lord Jesus Christ. 3 Blessed be the God and Father of our Lord Jesus Christ, who hath blessed us with all spiritual blessings in heavenly places in Christ:
Ephesians 1:2 - 3

On the basis of the finished works of Christ, these saints had already been blessed with all spiritual blessings in heavenly places in Christ. Heavenly places refer to Christ. It is not some location outside Christ. Christ is the believer's heavenly places. All spiritual blessings are secure in Him. There is no saint that is not already blessed with all spiritual blessings in Christ. Its just that there are too many that don't know what they have in the gift of the new spirit.

How do you minister to those that have been blessed with all spiritual blessings in Christ but are not laying hold of it? We help them by laying hands on those who do not know how to make use of what they already have in the indwelling of the holy ghost. Paul ministered to them by laying on of hands. His laying on of hands was not giving them anything that wasn't already theirs in Christ. Paul laid hands on them because laying on of hands is a secondary means of awakening the believer to what is his or hers in Christ. The laying on of hands doesn't make God give anything that He has not already given in Christ. We lay hands as a bona fide way of helping people to receive. It tends to work when nothing else will.

Paul asked the Ephesian disciples an important question that we do well to understand also.

3 And he said unto them, Unto what then were ye baptized? And they said, Unto John's baptism. 4 Then said Paul, John verily baptized with the baptism of repentance, saying unto the people, that they should believe on him which should come after him, that is, on Christ Jesus. 5 When they heard this, they were baptized in the name of the Lord Jesus.
Acts 19:3 - 5

Paul's big question was, "Unto what then were ye baptized"?

Their response was, "Unto John's baptism".

The issue of John's baptism is not a trivial point in the book of Acts. This is what Peter told Cornelius about John's baptism:

37 That word, I say, ye know, which was published throughout all Judaea, and began from Galilee, after the baptism which John preached; 38 How God anointed Jesus of Nazareth with the Holy Ghost and with power: who went about doing good, and healing all that were oppressed of the devil; for God was with him.
Acts 10:37 - 38

Peter informed Cornelius that the baptism of John was a baptism which John preached. We have been schooled into seeing water anytime we see the word baptism as though baptism means water. However, the dominant act of that John's baptism was not the dipping into water but its doctrine.

Although John used water, John's baptism was a teaching.

The thing that began at John's baptism was that God anointed Jesus. When a man receives the gift of holy spirit he is said to be anointed (see Acts 10:38). This fact that God had anointed Jesus was the word which was published throughout all Judaea, and began from Galilee, after the baptism. From that point onwards, the teaching of Jesus and His disciples was that God had anointed Jesus. God anointed Jesus by giving Him the spirit without measure. The anointing is not a separate thing from the spirit.

Observe that Peter then went beyond John's baptism in his message to Cornelius.

And we are witnesses of all things which he did both in the land of the Jews, and in Jerusalem; whom they slew and hanged on a tree: 40Him God raised up the third day, and shewed him openly; 41 Not to all the people, but unto witnesses chosen before of God, even to us, who did eat and drink with him after he rose from the dead. 42 And he commanded us to preach unto the people, and to testify that it is he which was ordained of God to be the Judge of quick and dead. 43To him give all the prophets witness, that through his name whosoever believeth in him shall receive remission of sins.

Acts 10:39 - 43

The teaching called John's baptism was promissory, for it told of what could be but could not proclaim it as accomplished. It was a shadow of things to come. John was not alive to proclaim its fulfilment. The teaching of John's baptism could not state as accomplished fact, the death of Jesus by hanging on a tree, or how God had raised Jesus up from the dead on the third day, or the fact that as a consequence, God had appointed Him the Judge of the quick and the dead or how by believing in Him, people could receive the actual remission of sins.

What Peter preached to Cornelius was apostolic teaching for the Church age. Peter's teaching went beyond John's baptism. Peter preached that men could believe in order to receive the New Birth which is the gift of the holy spirit given by the Lord Jesus.

In choosing Judas' replacement, before the day of Pentecost, this is what Peter said to the disciples in reference to John's baptism:

Beginning from the baptism of John, unto that same day that he was taken up from us, must one be ordained to be a witness with us of his resurrection.
Acts 1:22

The Baptism of John referred to the beginning of Jesus ministry. This refers to Jesus' revelation to Israel as the Anointed One through John's ministry and goes all the way till He gave up Himself as the sacrifice for sins.

Peter's expression "that same day that he was taken up from us" was not a reference to His earth walk as an anointed minister to Israel but to His redemption work culminating in His ascension after His resurrection.

Peter was saying that Judas' replacement needed to have a two-fold revelation. The first was that received through the ministry of John. The second was the fulfilment in His resurrection.

We can see more details about John's baptism in the record of Apollos at Ephesus.

Knowing only the baptism of John

24 And a certain Jew named Apollos, born at Alexandria, an eloquent man, and mighty in the scriptures, came to Ephesus. 25 This man was instructed in the way of the Lord; and being fervent in the spirit, he spake and taught diligently the things of the Lord, knowing only the baptism of John.
Acts 18:24 - 25

Apollos was described as "knowing only the baptism of John." This confirms that the baptism of John was a body of knowledge that John taught. Moreover, Luke speaks about John's baptism as though it was incomplete by itself. The language is "knowing only the baptism of John." It is as if there was more. There was something greater. Apollos' instruction in the way of the Lord was his knowledge of the baptism of John. Apollos was so grounded in John's baptism that it was said of him that "he spake and taught diligently the things of the Lord." This shows that the baptism of John is a level of insight into the things of the Lord. It is the revelation of Jesus that John had taught to his disciples. The baptism of John is a shadow of something greater.

26 And he began to speak boldly in the synagogue: whom when Aquila and Priscilla had heard, they took him unto them, and expounded unto him the way of God more perfectly.
Acts 18:26

When Aquila and Priscilla had heard Apollos teach his insight into the things of the Lord from the perspective of John's baptism, they could decipher from what they heard him say that there were gaps that needed being filled. Aquila and Priscilla then expounded unto Apollos the way of God more perfectly.

What could this "the way of God more perfectly" refer to? Since this is contrasted to John's baptism, the more perfect explanation would likely be a greater baptism. They likely told Apollos that by His finished works, the Lord Jesus had supplied a greater and enduring baptism which fulfilled what John started to teach.

This means that just like Peter had taught Cornelius, Aquila and Priscilla taught Apollos a revelation of Jesus beyond John's baptism. As a result of this, Apollos received more light about the greater baptism that is supplied in Christ Jesus.

27 And when he was disposed to pass into Achaia, the brethren wrote, exhorting the disciples to receive him: who, when he was come, helped them much which had believed through grace: 28 For he mightily convinced the Jews, and that publicly, shewing by the scriptures that Jesus was Christ.
Acts 18:27 - 28

Aquila and Priscilla were products of the ministry of Paul, who was a strong teacher of God's grace through the finished works of Christ. They used the scriptures to furnish Apollos with revelation knowledge that caused Apollos' knowledge of Jesus to go from Jordan to the throne. It was after Aquila and Priscilla had expounded unto Apollos the way of God more perfectly that grace was associated with Apollos' teaching. He had come in contact with the revelation of God's grace in Christ Jesus. He now knew that the Lord had supplied the promised rivers of living water by giving the gift of holy spirit from the Father's right hand.

Now, Apollos could convincingly show by the scriptures that Jesus was Christ. Apollos' teaching would be approximately the same as Jesus' Emmaus teaching that He had given to the disciples after His resurrection.

44 And he said unto them, These are the words which I spake unto you, while I was yet with you, that all things must be fulfilled, which were written in the law of Moses, and in the prophets, and in the psalms, concerning me. 45 Then opened he their understanding, that they might understand the scriptures, 46 And said unto them, Thus it is written, and thus it behoved Christ to suffer, and to rise from the dead the third day

Luke 24: 44 - 46

Up till this point, all that the disciples of Jesus knew was the doctrine called John's Baptism. Now, fresh from His resurrection, Jesus opened the understanding of the disciples so that they could understand the scriptures properly. Jesus basically told them that He had fulfilled those things which were written in the law of Moses, and in the prophets, and in the Psalms. It is done! It is finished! It is settled!

Apollos "knowing John's baptism" means that Apollos knew of the Lord Jesus up till His anointing and proclamation by John to Israel as the Lamb who was to take away the sins of the world.

John the Baptist died before prophecy became fact. Therefore, at best, John was a pre-resurrection saint who trusted in what the Lord would do. John couldn't say, "Done"! As a result, anyone who was baptised into John would believe Jesus to be the Lamb of God but would be unaware that the promise had been fulfilled in His resurrection and that the Lord Jesus had given the promised new spirit as His permanent gift to those who believe. Those that know "only John's baptism" would be unaware of the heavenly ministry of the Lord Jesus. Jesus' resurrection and sitting rendered the teaching of John's baptism an incomplete message that did not capture the way of the Lord fully. Aquila and Priscilla filled in these gaps for Apollos by taking his knowledge from the baptism of John, which is the anointing of Jesus, to the knowledge of Jesus' death, burial, resurrection and seating in heaven. It would mean telling a man that the spirit is given for the Lord is glorified!

Apollos' knowledge of the Lord would be more complete; thus, he would be able to believe that the death and resurrection were no longer prophecies but fact. Apollos would then fulfil the condition for receiving the New Birth. By believing in his heart that God had raised Jesus from the dead as well as confessing His Lordship with his mouth, Apollos would receive the power from on high, which is the permanent gift of the holy spirit as his nature (see Romans 10:8). At that point, using the language of Acts, Apollos believed in the name of the Lord and would have been baptised into the name of Jesus. Baptism into the name of Jesus means that Apollos believed all that Jesus had accomplished in redemption.

The greater baptism

There is a strong similarity between Priscilla and Aquila's ministry to Apollos and Paul's ministry to the Ephesians. Both Apollos and the Ephesus group were founded on the teaching called John's baptism.

He said unto them, Have ye received the Holy Ghost since ye believed? And they said unto him, We have not so much as heard whether there be any Holy Ghost.
3 And he said unto them, Unto what then were ye baptized? And they said,
Unto John's baptism. 4 Then said Paul, John verily baptized with the baptism
of repentance, saying unto the people, that they should believe on him which
should come after him, that is, on Christ Jesus. 5 When they heard this, they

were baptized in the name of the Lord Jesus.
Acts 19:2 - 5

When Paul asked his big question, "Unto what then were ye baptized?" and the disciples responded, "Unto John's baptism", they were not referring to water. John's baptism meant that they were unaware that Christ's death and resurrection were no longer prophecies but fact. They did not know that Christ had been glorified at the Father's hand in heaven, from where He supplied the permanent gift of holy spirit.

John the Baptist spoke of Jesus and of the Holy Ghost. However, these Ephesian disciples did not know whether there was a holy ghost. They had received a watered-down version of John's baptism!

4 Then said Paul, John verily baptized with the baptism of repentance, saying unto the people, that they should believe on him which should come after him, that is, on Christ Jesus.
Acts 19:4

Notice that according to Paul, John's baptism of repentance was summed up in what John said to the people. John's baptism was his saying about Christ Jesus. The baptism of John was known by its saying or teaching and by extension, what his hearers should have believed as a result of his teaching.

Paul used the things that John had taught, by his baptism, as foundation for teaching the Ephesians the revelation of Christ. John's water baptism was a shadow of the greater work of Christ, which would supply the greater baptism.

When Paul asked, "Unto what were you baptised?", he was asking them, "What have you heard or believed?"

That which a person has been baptised into summarises what that person has been taught and therefore believed.

5 When they heard this, they were baptized in the name of the Lord Jesus. 6
And when Paul had laid his hands upon them, the Holy Ghost came on them;

and they spake with tongues, and prophesied.
Acts 19:5 - 6

Paul expounded more fully the way of the Lord to the Ephesian disciples by "Beginning from the baptism of John" and teaching them the redemption realities that culminated in His being "taken up from us" in order to send the promised spirit to us.

No specific river or stream is mentioned; therefore, we mustn't dilute the message with water. That which a person has been baptised into summarises what that person has been taught and therefore believed.

This expression "When they heard this, they were baptized in the name of the Lord Jesus", means that they believed what Paul had taught them that Jesus' name represents. In simple terms, they had heard and believed Paul's revelation of Christ, which took them from Jordan and went all the way to the throne and the gift given from the throne. It is critical that people understand that the Father has glorified the Lord and that as a result, Jesus has received the promise from the Father and given the promised power from on high to men as the new spirit in the born-again experience.

Receiving the riches of Christ

The first three chapters of Ephesians give us a clue concerning what the Ephesians were baptised into. Those chapters are a continual revelation of what God has done in us by His Son.

2 If ye have heard of the dispensation of the grace of God which is given me to you-ward: 3 How that by revelation he made known unto me the mystery; (as I wrote afore in few words, 4 Whereby, when ye read, ye may understand my knowledge in the mystery of Christ)
Ephesians 3: 2 - 4

Paul taught the revelation of what God had accomplished in Christ to the Ephesian saints and then wrote that revelation down in order that our understanding might be enriched in that knowledge. According to that revelation, God has made us saints, set us apart for Himself and already blessed us with all spiritual blessings in the heavenlies in Christ (see Ephesians 1:3). There was nothing extra that God needed to give them because all the spiritual blessings that there was to be given is already given to the saint in Christ Jesus when Christ gave the promised holy spirit.

This is by God for God. We do nothing apart from receiving the riches.

We did not initiate God accepting us in the beloved and choosing us in Christ, He did (see Ephesians 1:4). No matter how hard we tried, there is not anything more that we could do to make Him accept us (see Ephesians 1:4). In Him we already have redemption, which is the forgiveness of sins, once and for all (see Ephesians 1:7).

He raised us when He raised Christ. Therefore, our resurrection is just as glorious and as certain as that of Christ Jesus'. It was a joint resurrection in Him. He has also already made us to sit together with Him far above all principalities and powers (see Ephesians 2:6). As if any of that was not enough, He assures us of His power at work within us (see Ephesians 3:20).

As you read through the first three chapters of Paul's letter to the Ephesians, you'll observe that the saint is not told to do anything. There is nothing for you to do. The first three chapters tell us that we have been made to sit together with Christ. We identify with and belong in His coronation. Those first three chapters are a declaration of what has already been done by the Father. God is flexing Himself as a Father and the believing one is the beneficiary of the Father's flexing.

Its language is "this is what God has done".

32 He that spared not his own Son, but delivered him up for us all, how shall he not with him also freely give us all things?
Romans 8: 32

All that God gave to us, He gave freely. There were no strings attached. The fact is that God has freely given us all things in Christ. We are not trying to talk Him into giving us utterance for all is already given to us in Christ.

God has given everything in that He gave the gift of holy spirit, which is God's divine nature, to Christ. Christ then gives that spirit as His gift to the saint. The gift of holy spirit is the crowning act of the Lord Jesus Christ's exaltation at the Father's right hand. Our minds must not wander from the fact that all spiritual blessings have already been given in Christ and that the blessing is in us as the gift of holy spirit.

20 Now unto him that is able to do exceeding abundantly above all that we ask or think, according to the power that worketh in us, 21 Unto him be glory in the church by Christ Jesus throughout all ages, world without end. Amen.
Ephesians 3: 20 - 21

It is as though the book of Ephesians is Paul writing two letters in one. He closes up his thoughts at the end of chapter three. He then picks up something fresh in chapter four onwards.

1 I therefore, the prisoner of the Lord, beseech you that ye walk worthy of the vocation wherewith ye are called,
Ephesians 4: 1

After four chapters, he says that he wants the Church to know how to walk. He does not tell the Christian to do anything until he has clearly established that the Christian has been made to sit in Him. He wants us to be certain about what He has done in us. We are walking and taking our stand because we know that He has made us to sit. We are walking and standing from that enviable position – He has made us sit. Walking and standing describe the responsibility that goes with His making us to sit in Him.

Paul is beseeching through the information that he has given to us concerning what has already been accomplished in Christ. It is not an empty plea. In the last three chapters of Ephesians, the saint who is chosen, accepted, sealed and blessed with all spiritual blessings needs to walk and stand in the power of the spirit! Saints do not try to re-do what is already done, nor do they try to talk God into doing them again.

Paul wants us to see that spiritual growth is not a finished work of Christ. We are walking worthy of God's phenomenal workings as recorded in the first three chapters of Ephesians. As saints, we walk worthy of that which the Father has already done by taking our stand in the power of God's might which is in the gift of holy spirit.

The revelation of the power of God's might which is in the gift of holy spirit is to translate to a consciousness of how we walk as well as stand.

6 And when Paul had laid his hands upon them, the Holy Ghost came on them; and they spake with tongues, and prophesied.
Acts 19: 6

Paul preached the revelation of Christ contained in the first three chapters of Ephesians to them in order to help them see what is already done in Christ. When people can see what Christ has done, it is much easier for them to take hold of the spiritual blessings that are guaranteed in Christ and speak with tongues and prophesy.

All true pneumatology is rooted in a sound Christology.

8

YE MAY UNDERSTAND

9 Receiving the end of your faith, even the salvation of your souls. 10 Of which salvation the prophets have enquired and searched diligently, who prophesied of the grace that should come unto you: 11 Searching what, or what manner of time the Spirit of Christ which was in them did signify, when it testified beforehand the sufferings of Christ, and the glory that should follow. 12 Unto whom it was revealed, that not unto themselves, but unto us they did minister the things, which are now reported unto you by them that have preached the gospel unto you with the Holy Ghost sent down from heaven; which things the angels desire to look into.

1 Peter 1:9 - 12

It was by the operation of the holy spirit upon the Old Testament prophets that they prophesied of the future sufferings of Christ and the glory that should follow that suffering. God communicated revelation to them by His gift of holy spirit. These prophets then spoke by the manifestation of the spirit called word of wisdom. The prophesies which were spoken by the operation of the holy spirit upon the Old Testament prophets, when written down, became scriptures.

Although they spoke in their generation, they did not minister these things to themselves or the generations that lived prior to the coming of Christ. Since they did not minister unto themselves, they did not receive edification from their utterances. The reason was because they did not understand what they were prophesying out of their mouths. These revelations came to them as inspiration but they did not really understand them.

A major difference between the gift of spirit upon the saints of the Church age and the Old Testament prophets in relation to the manifestation of the spirit is that the gift of holy spirit given after Christ's exaltation, is so radically different that it communicates the life of God, which carries with it the comprehension of the things ministered by utterance. The glory that should follow the sufferings of Christ was the spirit that Christ gave at His exaltation. That spirit is the capacity to fully understand the plan of God. The saints of the Church age are to operate in the understanding of the prophecies that the Old Testament prophets did not understand although they accurately prophesied.

13 Wherefore gird up the loins of your mind, be sober, and hope to the end for the grace that is to be brought unto you at the revelation of Jesus Christ
1 Peter 1:13

Peter's admonition to the saints in the Church age "gird up the loins of your mind, be sober" means that the saints in the Church age would properly receive, understand and minister the things that the prophets had prophesied. We can minister our understanding of the prophetic scriptures for the Word tells us that the object of these prophecies is Christ. We proclaim the revelation of Jesus Christ as the foundation and explanation of all things. The revelation of Jesus is not just inspirational to us, we are meant to understand it.

When all the Old Testament prophets prophesied of Christ, although their mouth had spoken it, their hearts did not have an understanding of what they had prophesied out of their own mouths. What was prophetic and futuristic for them, the saints of the Church age declare as done and already accomplished in Christ Jesus.

Real spiritual understanding does not come by speaking a word of wisdom. Scriptural understanding comes to the mind through reading and studying scriptures as well as hearing it get taught. Clarity, certainty and less scratching of heads is a product of diligent study. We only come to understand that which we have previously spoken by inspiration as we expose our minds to the written Word.

The prophecies that these Old Testament Prophets spoke out of their own mouths by the inspiration of the Holy Spirit were dark sayings and parables both to the speakers as well as the hearers.

Visions are not untouchable

18 And this voice which came from heaven we heard, when we were with him in the holy mount. 19 We have also a more sure word of prophecy; whereunto ye do well that ye take heed, as unto a light that shineth in a dark place, until the day dawn, and the day star arise in your hearts:
2 Peter 1:18 - 19

Peter prioritized the more sure Word above the audible voice that he had heard from heaven. The more sure Word is the written Word, which is the light shining in the dark place giving understanding to the mind. Thus, the scriptures are a more sure means of giving understanding to the saints than visions and prophecies. The clarity accessible through the written Word is infinitely more than that contained within visions, voices, trances or any other spiritual experiences. It is the insight that we receive through the written Word that we use to administer and understand spiritual manifestations. The depth of insight contained in a pure vision is no match for that available from reading the scriptures. Visions are not untouchable. There would be significantly less confusion in the Church if we used our understanding of the Word to examine visions.

Peter's vision in Acts 10 illustrates that visions are excellent channels for receiving directions but poor for imparting doctrine.

9 On the morrow, as they went on their journey, and drew nigh unto the city,

Peter went up upon the housetop to pray about the sixth hour: 10 And he became very hungry, and would have eaten: but while they made ready, he fell into a trance, 11 And saw heaven opened, and a certain vessel descending upon him, as it had been a great sheet knit at the four corners, and let down to the earth: 12 Wherein were all manner of fourfooted beasts of the earth, and wild beasts, and creeping things, and fowls of the air. 13 And there came a voice to him, Rise, Peter; kill, and eat. 14 But Peter said, Not so, Lord; for I have never eaten any thing that is common or unclean.15 And the voice spake unto him again the second time, What God hath cleansed, that call not thou common. 16 This was done thrice: and the vessel was received up again into heaven. 17 Now while Peter doubted in himself what this vision which he had seen should mean, behold, the men which were sent from Cornelius had made enquiry for Simon's house, and stood before the gate, 18 And called, and asked whether Simon, which was surnamed Peter, were lodged there. 19 While Peter thought on the vision, the Spirit said unto him, Behold, three men seek thee. 20 Arise therefore, and get thee down, and go with them, doubting nothing: for I have sent them.
Acts 10:9 - 20

Interestingly, God commanded Cornelius through the angel to send for the man Peter, who would tell Cornelius what to do (see Acts 10:6). The angel standing in Cornelius' presence did not have insight into the gospel. The angels would understand salvation by observing Peter and their understanding of it would improve as Peter gets better at sharing the gospel. Angels use men to interpret the will of God. Men are the classroom of angels.

In the vision, Peter said, "Not so, Lord." He knew it was the Lord, yet he still said no! Many years after Peter had spoken in tongues at Pentecost, his mind was still not renewed to the Lord's way of reasoning. This shows that Peter did not need perfect theology in order to manifest the spirit by speaking in tongues.

Peter had fallen into a trance and then seen a vision. This was a very clear vision. Peter could accurately describe the geometry - It was a great sheet with four corners. Inside this sheet, Peter could see four-footed beasts as well as other types of animals. Peter saw both kosher animals and non-kosher animals. Although the vision showed animals, its scope was about concepts that were of a wider application than animals. The voice that spoke to Peter wanted him to realise what the Lord had done by Himself in providing salvation through faith, which is in Christ. The Lord that had cleansed that which Peter still referred to as common. Peter was a saint who was still drunk on the Law. He was blind to the fact that the Lord Jesus, by His death and resurrection put the Law away and had cleansed the gentiles.

After this spectacular trance, Peter doubted in himself what this vision which he had seen should mean. This means that Peter struggled to understand the message contained in that vision. Seeing a vision does not confer insight or increase knowledge apart from the written Word. The written Word would have removed the cobb-webs in Peter's mind and freed his mind to receive and grasp the truth contained within that vision. Peter's doubts shows that crystal-clear visions must not be confused with razor sharp understanding of the message of the vision!

Since the gift of holy spirit that Peter received at the New Birth is complete in Christ and one with the Lord, Peter's spirit would not be at odds with the Lord. Therefore, Peter's spirit did not need that vision. It was Peter's mind, which had been trained in the Law, that was resisting the transformation that was coming via the gift of holy spirit which indwelt him. Peter's mind was more conformed to the traditions of the Law than to the spirit through the written Word.

If Peter's mind had been renewed to the Old Testament prophecies he would not have needed that vision. If his mind was full of the content of those prophecies, he would have the raw materials for gaining understanding of what the vision meant.

Arise, shine; for thy light is come, and the glory of the Lord is risen upon thee. 2 For, behold, the darkness shall cover the earth, and gross darkness the people: but the Lord shall arise upon thee, and his glory shall be seen upon thee. 3 And the Gentiles shall come to thy light, and kings to the brightness of thy rising.
Isaiah 60:1 - 3

Isaiah's prophecy, "Gentiles shall come to thy light", contained the permission that Peter needed in order to go with the men that had come from Cornelius. That prophecy would supply the understanding to the revelation contained within Peter's vision. Peter's vision was not communicating anything new to Peter that he could not have read in the holy scriptures! Isaiah did not have a recreated spirit; therefore, he would have scratched his head when he gave that prophecy. However, Peter should have understood the vision, if he had been a man of the Word.

Peter was effectively operating like the prophets who had ministered before Christ. He had much inspiration via that vision but not much understanding. The truths contained within Peter's vision are easily understood by the saints reading the Pauline Epistles.

Understanding through the written Word

3 How that by revelation he made known unto me the mystery; (as I wrote afore in few words, 4 Whereby, when ye read, ye may understand my knowledge in the mystery of Christ) 5 Which in other ages was not made known unto the sons of men, as it is now revealed unto his holy apostles and prophets by the Spirit
Ephesians 3:3 - 5

Paul's reason for writing the Epistles was so that "when ye read, ye may understand." Thus, the Lord does not require His saints to fall into trances and see visions like Peter in order to grasp doctrinal matters. Saints are called to understand by reading the clearly stated truths of redemption. It is by reading the written Word that revelation progresses from inspiration to becoming knowledge and understanding to the saints. The understanding that comes to the mind through reading the written Word is second to none.

Prior to Christ supplying the New Birth, the prophets spoke the mystery of Christ in various words of knowledge and words of wisdom, which they later wrote down as scriptures. The meaning of their utterances was hidden from them for it contained the wisdom of God for the salvation of man. By hiding it from men, God was keeping

His strategy hidden from the devil, the slanderer, who had the power of death (see Matthew 16:23; 1 Corinthians 2:7-8; Hebrews 2:14). Although these prophets were speaking secrets concerning Christ out of their mouths, no matter how much they diligently searched, these secrets were hidden from their understanding and their spirits (see 1 Peter 1:10-11). It was successfully hid from the spirits of men in previous because until the resurrection of Jesus, there were no born again men. Spiritual death hindered man's spirit from being able to receive the understanding of the mystery.

Interestingly these prophets had understanding when their word of wisdom concerned things about people other than Christ. However, whenever they spoke concerning Christ, their understanding was veiled by spiritual death.

Observe that unlike those Old Testament prophets, who were not born again, Paul did not just get a revelation of the mystery; he also had knowledge of that revelation. This was because Paul had received the gift of holy spirit and he had allowed that gift illuminate the truths of the written Word to him. Paul's writings were structured to give understanding to the Church concerning his knowledge of the revelation of the mystery. His writing was his explanation of the various words of wisdom and words of knowledge of the prophets of the past ages.

The monumental difference between what had been hidden from the prophets and what is now knowledge to the saints is the finished work of Christ, which has provided the New Birth in the form of the new spirit in man. The gift of holy spirit gives the saint the capacity to understand what the Lord has done from the same scriptures that had confused the old saints.

Until the Lord Jesus provided redemption and sat down at the Father's right hand, there was no degree of spiritual diligence or growth that anyone could exercise that could produce the New birth or make a man speak in tongues. This explains why even after His resurrection, while Jesus was on earth but before he sat down at the Father's right hand, no man on earth could get born again since Jesus had not received the gift of the holy spirit from the Father, in an indwelling measure, to give to men.

God's masterful plan of salvation was being established through their prophecies but they didn't understand it. We do not minister all the prophecies of these prophets. It is the gospel content of their written prophecies, which is the revelation of Jesus Christ that the saints of the Church age are to minister and preach.

This idea that the Old Testament prophets flowed strongly in inspiration without understanding their own utterances about Christ is readily observable in the interaction of John the Baptist with Jesus.

28 For I say unto you, Among those that are born of women there is not a greater prophet than John the Baptist: but he that is least in the kingdom of God is greater than he.
Luke 7: 28

John is a particularly important example, since Jesus rated John highly as the most advanced prophet of the Old Testament. When we see John in action, we are observing the height of the Old Testament prophetic ministry.

32 And John bare record, saying, I saw the Spirit descending from heaven like a dove, and it abode upon him.33 And I knew him not: but he that sent me to baptize with water, the same said unto me, Upon whom thou shalt see the Spirit descending, and remaining on him, the same is he which baptizeth with the Holy Ghost. 34 And I saw, and bare record that this is the Son of God.
John 1:32 - 33

John was the greatest Old Testament prophet because he gave the most accurate word of knowledge and word of wisdom in the entire bible by directly identifying Christ Jesus as the Lamb of God. John the Baptist did not claim to have come about this revelation by understanding scriptures. He saw a vision that confirmed to him that Jesus is the Son of God. He knew by observing the sign that the spirit had given him - in a vision He saw the spirit descend upon Christ.

God had said that John would see the spirit descend and remain upon

Jesus. Yet, when John testified of the vision that he saw, he said, "I saw the Spirit descending from heaven like a dove, and it abode upon him" (see John 1:32). Notice that God had said nothing about a dove. It was John who uniquely added "like a dove" to what God had said. When the spirit came upon men at Pentecost or at any other time in the book of Acts, Luke made no mention of a dove. It wasn't that God forgot to tell John about the dove. The reason why God had not informed John about the dove was because there was no dove present. Although many wish it were so, the Spirit is not a dove, nor is the dove the symbol of the Spirit. John just had something for doves. If you had been the one who had seen this vision, you would most likely not have said "like a dove". You would have used a different expression to convey the same point.

John's expression "like a dove", shows that what we see in a vision and how we describe it are not necessarily the same thing. John described the vision using his own words at his level of understanding. Although God had given John a vision, John's conscience or understanding introduced the dove as an element of the overall experience. You would also describe your visions using your own language. John is to be commended for correctly identifying Jesus to Israel as the promised One.

19 And John calling unto him two of his disciples sent them to Jesus, saying, Art thou he that should come? or look we for another?
Luke 7:19

Observe that although John had correctly identified Jesus as the Lamb of God, much later he sent people to ask Jesus, "Art thou he that should come? or look we for another"? At that point in time, John was not speaking by inspiration but from his understanding. This was the true question in John's mind when he was not seeing God-granted visions. Thus, much earlier, when John had declared, "Behold the lamb of God", he was speaking by the gift of spirit upon him as he fulfilled the ministry of a prophet. When he spoke out the word of wisdom as prophecy, he was not speaking out his understanding. Since John did not know this fact by the understanding, clarity and assurance that comes from scripture, we readily see that he knew what he knew about Jesus taking away the sins of the world by the word of wisdom. John's knowledge about Jesus was knowledge via the things that he had seen in a vision, when he had seen the spirit descend upon Jesus.

Until the Lord Jesus accomplished redemption, not even John the Baptist, could minister to another that the sins of the world had been taken away. The depth of revelation knowledge that John could proclaim was limited by time itself. What those standing around John needed at that point in time was the unveiling of the Lamb to Israel. After the resurrection of Jesus, the revelation of what He had done would be needful.

We can apply these concepts to speaking in tongues.

The mind, the mouth and tongues

2 For he that speaketh in an unknown tongue speaketh not unto men, but unto God: for no man understandeth him; howbeit in the spirit he speaketh mysteries.
1 Corinthians 14:2

The NASB correctly translates this as "for no man understands". This means that the mind of the speaker in tongues does not understand the religious secrets that he is saying when he speaks in other tongues. If the person speaking in tongues is a native Russian speaker, such a person's tongues cannot be Russian. If it were, the sounds cannot be called other tongues. There is nothing that says that there might not be someone present who understands what is being said; although typically, no one present understands the sounds spoken. In practice, you'll find that when mature saints are gathered together and all are speaking in tongues, you don't tend to have any of them understanding the dialect that was spoken by another as other tongues. In order to understand what has been spoken in tongues, another manifestation of the spirit known as the interpretation of tongues would come into operation.

Speaking in tongues is an activity of the human spirit where the speaker willingly and deliberately continues to push out non-familiar sounds from the mouth through the vocal chords. When we speak religious secrets in tongues, our minds hear these sounds. Although, our mouths are releasing these sounds, its meaning does not register on our minds or the minds of those who hear us. In that sense, the mind and mouth are like the Old Testament prophet speaking secrets that were hidden from the mind of the speaker. By another manifestation of the spirit, the spirit then restates the sounds spoken out in tongues on a level that the mind can grasp.

The moment of grasping by the mind is not the moment that revelation came. We speak in tongues to convey the revelation that is already within our spirits. There is no requirement to always interpret tongues. Tongues are always to be interpreted in public meetings. When we interpret, we are restating the revelation, in a language known to the mind, in order that the mind might be enabled to receive the understanding of the revelation. Interpretation brings understanding which makes the things spoken more sure to the mind. Interpretation of tongues is not for the benefit of the spirit of the speaker. Interpretation does nothing for the spirit. It is for the mind.

Utterance comes through the human spirit in the form of inspiration to speak. We respond to that inspiration by speaking religious secrets or mysteries. When we speak these religious secrets in private, they directly supply edification to us. However, if spoken in public assembly as a form of ministry, the religious secrets will only bring edification to others when interpreted.

16 Else when thou shalt bless with the spirit, how shall he that occupieth the room of the unlearned say Amen at thy giving of thanks, seeing he understandeth not what thou sayest? 17 For thou verily givest thanks well, but the other is not edified.
1 Corinthians 14: 16 - 17

It is unscriptural to publicly speak the edification meant for the

Church in tongues and leave the assembly unedified because we did not follow up with the manifestation of the interpretation of tongues. If we operated that way, the saints for whom Christ died would be like the Eunuch who was perplexed by Isaiah's prophecy, while the speaker in tongues would be like the Old Testament prophet having a head-scratching moment. Religious secrets would have been spoken but the understanding of it would have been withheld from the mind of the saints.

The one occupying the room of the unlearned cannot receive the edification contained within speaking in tongues because he does not understand what has been spoken in tongues. The unlearned are unable to say amen to the good thing spoken in tongues because the speaker in tongues is untaught about the proper exercise and administration of spiritual flow.

Paul's major point here is that it is possible to experience speaking in tongues but not understand that it is the same spirit that manifests tongues that manifests interpretation of tongues. It is up to the speaker in tongues to bless others by using tongues as the tool for bringing edification, exhortation and comfort to the Church by interpreting the tongue.

19 Yet in the church I had rather speak five words with my understanding, that by my voice I might teach others also, than ten thousand words in an unknown tongue.

1 Corinthians 14: 19

Although, interpretation of tongues is more pronounced in public ministry of tongues, the speaker in tongues should be able to exercise interpretation of tongues in the private life when needed. The ability to receive or give maximum benefit from tongues, in public or private life, flows from your understanding through the Word that tongues and interpretation of tongues are manifestations of the same spirit. The more ignorant we are about the sufficiency of God in the spirit of man, the less effective we are in interpreting our tongues even if we flow in speaking in tongues.

We are to seek to manifest utterance with such mastery that we can say together with Paul, "that by my voice I might teach others also." Since the speaker in tongues is the one teaching others also, we must appreciate that it is up to the speaker in tongues to bless others by using tongues as the tool for bringing edification to the Church. The edification can come forth as a teaching. This means that it is as we explain things to the saints in order to enrich their understanding that the saints receive edification. The only reason for the existence of public ministry of tongues is so that it might be interpreted.

Who needs understanding?

3 Wherefore I give you to understand, that no man speaking by the Spirit of God calleth Jesus accursed: and that no man can say that Jesus is the Lord, but by the Holy Ghost.
1 Corinthians 12: 3

Paul is using his letter as the vehicle for giving further understanding about the abilities of the new spirit to the saints. The Corinthians had already seen and heard supernatural flow experientially. Now, Paul writes to the saints so that by reading they might receive deeper understanding of that which they already experienced.

Teaching gives understanding to those who already manifest the spirit.

27 But the anointing which ye have received of him abideth in you, and ye need not that any man teach you: but as the same anointing teacheth you of all things, and is truth, and is no lie, and even as it hath taught you, ye shall abide in him.
1 John 2: 27

This anointing that we received of Him is the gift of the holy spirit which teaches us all things by the new nature.

Since the spirit of man is born of the incorruptible seed of God's Word at the New Birth, the Word and the human spirit are one (see

1 Peter 1:23). Therefore, the new nature does not need to be taught. Instead, that nature teaches.

Is John contradicting himself by teaching the saints when he already established that we need not that any man teaches us?

John describes how to protect the mind of the saint from deception. The new nature inoculates the mind against deception by bringing understanding to the mind through the written Word. When we teach the Word, we are not teaching the human spirit. We are energising the eyes of his understanding so that he might know. We teach because the mind of the saint receives understanding via teaching.

12 Now we have received, not the spirit of the world, but the spirit which is of God; that we might know the things that are freely given to us of God.
1 Corinthians 2: 12

The gift of holy spirit that the Lord Jesus gave to us at the New Birth causes us to know all the things that are freely given to us of God. The human spirit might not know the weather pattern in Sri Lanka but it knows all the riches of Christ.

John's statement about not needing any man to teach you is a reference to the anointing of man with the holy spirit at the New Birth. John is teaching the abilities of the spirit to the mind of the saints, in order that they might be established in that reality. This is because the human mind must be transformed to cooperate with the spirit. Therefore, both teaching and reading are needed for the mind to receive the understanding that the spirit already received at the New Birth.

9

THE COMMAND OF THE LORD

The matter of utterance ought not be a mystery to the Church. The spiritual experiences of the saints should be birthed by the Word, explained by the Word and sustained by the Word. I have been surprised by the scarcity of materials on a matter so pivotal to the Christian. What is more baffling is that the Word is not silent on the matter of manifesting the spirit through utterance.

20 Despise not prophesyings. 21 Prove all things; hold fast that which is good.
1 Thessalonians 5: 20 - 21

We are commanded by the Apostle Paul to "prove all things; hold fast that which is good." His context was prophecy.

We are to prove those things that have to do with utterance. This does not mean that we should watch out for those things that are not cool about the manifestation of God's free gift, the holy spirit.

Ordinarily, the Lord conveys revelation to His saints by His gift of holy spirit. What He reveals becomes a prophecy when we minister it in a known language to the assembly for their edification. Prophecy is a manifestation of the spirit where the saint speaks forth a knowing that the Lord Jesus has conveyed to him or her through His gift of holy spirit within us. However, this is not always the case. If the Lord

Jesus conveyed the prophecy to the saint through the ministry of an angel, that wouldn't be classified as manifestation of the spirit since the mechanism of disclosure has not been the Lord through the human spirit. In that case, it wouldn't be the human spirit manifesting the prophecy. This book focuses on prophecy as a manifestation of the spirit. Such manifestation of prophecy would edify us by exhortation and comfort (see 1 Corinthians 14:3).

Although it is not immediately obvious, the vast majority of the prophecies that we give and receive concerning the future are conditional in nature because the slants, decisions and beliefs of the receiver of the prophecy influences its fulfilment. The conditional nature of prophecy is brought out clearly in Jonah's ministry to Nineveh. Jonah was emphatic, "yet forty days, and Nineveh shall be overthrown" (see Jonah 3:4). God's love and mercy moved Jonah and God used that prophecy to steer the people away from doom. Their repentance caused them to receive God's mercy and choke wrath; and as a consequence, doom was averted. That was a good thing that Jonah's prophecy did not come to pass. The repentance of Nineveh was God's will. We must not approach prophecies from a fatalistic mind-set and assume that whatever is prophesied is destined to happen – sometimes prophecies are spoken for the express purpose that they should fail (see Jeremiah 18:1-11).

Prophecies don't override the will of the people to whom they are spoken. On account of man's will, the general tone of scriptures is that by their responses, the receiver of a prophecy interacts with the prophecy to determine whether it will come to pass or not. The receiver would know what to do by prayer and meditation on the prophecy and on God's Word (see 2 Kings 20:1-6).

When Paul said to prove all things, he was letting us know that we are to prove that prophecy and utterance as well as other manifestations of the spirit are exactly as beneficial as they are written in the Word. Acting on this instruction would make us spirit scientists who experiment with the spiritual realities of our redemption. Paul wrote this to the Thessalonians as a collective because the local Church is the best theatre for the teaching and expression of the supernatural. It is within the context of the local Church that we can plumb the depths of the manifestation of the spirit. Therefore, it is within the local Church that you find these spirit engineers and scientists. These are men and women who are not afraid to experiment with the manifestation of the spirit in order to hold fast to the true gems of edification.

We are a Word Church. We must not be that kind of Word Church that are not also desirous of and intelligent in the flow of the Spirit. Any form of Word slant that plays down the importance of manifesting the spirit is pseudo-Word. That kind of Word Church is foreign to the scriptures.

Manifestation is up to the saint

18 I thank my God, I speak with tongues more than ye all:
1 Corinthians 14:18

Paul is strong on the matter of utterance. It is supremely important. He made it his duty to thank God for that which God has provided in Christ. Paul could see that speaking in tongues attested to God in a way that the sun, moon, seas and stars could not. He thanked God for that which bore the stamp of God's handiwork in redemption. The Lord Jesus is the author of His gift of holy spirit in man and He wants us to manifest that spirit by speaking in other tongues. Paul gave thanks to God concerning that. He did not thank God for anything else. Surprisingly, contrary to general practice in many quarters today, we don't find Paul, in any of his epistles thanking God for the visible or invisible universe. Those things never became the subject of his thanksgiving.

We are to thank God zealously and he spoke in tongues profusely. Paul thanked God that he spoke with tongues more than all the saints in the Corinthian Church. This wonderful boast would not amount to anything if Paul had been referring to the typical Church today. If people don't speak in tongues at all, it doesn't take much to say, "I speak in tongues more than you all." However, the Church in question is the Corinthian Church.

In order to appreciate the force of those words, you need to consider his testimony about the Corinthians:

4 I thank my God always on your behalf, for the grace of God which is given you by Jesus Christ;5 That in every thing ye are enriched by him, in all utterance, and in all knowledge;6 Even as the testimony of Christ was confirmed in you:7 So that ye come behind in no gift; waiting for the coming of our Lord Jesus Christ:

1 Corinthians 1:4-7

All saints have been enriched in all utterance and in all knowledge by Christ Jesus. Paul had taught the Corinthians so well about this divine deposit that they had responded by manifesting the spirit. Thus, they did not come behind in any gift.

The fact that Paul spoke in tongues more than the Corinthian Church that came behind in no gift, means that Paul must have been greatly exercised in the manifestation of the spirit. He was a disciple of utterance.

This idea that Paul could make this boast about the relative abundance of tongues through him in comparison to the Corinthians shows that the manifestation of the spirit can be counted and measured and that Paul was not neutral about such things. More importantly, it shows that the flow of the spirit in Paul was not the product of a sovereign move of God. If it was a sovereign move, then Paul had no right to affirm that he spoke in tongues more than they. Paul's boast lets us see that tongues is a faculty in his human spirit. It was like the linguistic capability of his human spirit. The comparison implied that the same linguistic faculty was also present in the saints in Corinth. Thus, the flow of the spirit could not have been a sovereign move in Paul, the Corinthians or any saint for that matter. The relative abundance of speaking in tongues in Paul compared to the Corinthians was down to the fact that he exercised his spiritual linguistics better than the Corinthian saints.

Today, unlearned saints will say,

"I thank my God, our cathedral and my Cadillac donkey are bigger than yours."

Paul's boast shows that we use the correct manifestation of the spirit to address any excess that we observe in spiritual flows. We don't withdraw in fear. He was looking to use his example to raise their awareness of the correct expression that they could follow. This re-affirms to us that the flow of the spirit in the Corinthian Church did not come by a sovereign move of God. It was not up to God who would flow and who would not. If you are still hung up on such terminologies as "moves of God", then the move of God is in the awareness that the teachings of Paul gave to the members of the Church. In simple terms, it is as saints become aware that "moves" start. It was the enrichment in knowledge concerning utterance that produced the avalanche of flow that was present in the Corinthian Church.

Paul's declaration helps us see that just as with any other language, the secret of fluency of tongues is to keep on speaking. The things of the spirit will not be pronounced if they are not taught and demonstrated.

The Spirit speaks expressly

Paul told Timothy, a fellow minister, "the Spirit speaketh expressly, that in the latter times some shall depart from the faith, giving heed to seducing spirits, and doctrines of devils" (see 1 Timothy 4:1). Paul did not just say, "The Spirit speaketh". He said, "The Spirit speaketh expressly". That Spirit is the Lord Jesus.

Paul's use of that term "expressly" qualifies how Paul received the Spirit's sayings. He was pressing home the point that the Lord Jesus, as the Head of the Church, was distinct and very clear in His dealings with Paul. It wasn't a hit-and-miss affair, nor was it fragmentary. The Spirit always speaks expressly; it is the saint that does not always perceive it distinctly in the mind.

It is true that Paul was first and foremost, a student of the Word. The Word made him a disciple of the correct expression of the supernatural. Paul was not shy to talk about the supernatural. Through Paul's ministry, the Lord Jesus gave clear instruction to the Corinthian Church about spirituals.

The Corinthian curriculum

1 And I, brethren, could not speak unto you as unto spiritual, but as unto carnal, even as unto babes in Christ.
1 Corinthians 3:1

All that are in Christ are in the spirit (see Romans 8:9); therefore, they are spiritual. Although these saints were all spiritual, these saints were walking in such a way that they were either addressed as "unto carnal" or as "unto spiritual". There was no middle ground. We are to think of the letters to Corinth as the curriculum for maturing "unto carnal" saints until they leave childish things and operate as "unto spiritual". Therefore, these precious letters to Corinth was Paul's apostolic method for growing immature Christians.

Today, the Church largely shuns teaching the curriculum that the Lord Jesus, as the life-giving Spirit, commissioned Paul to use to train His precious saints in Corinth.

2 I have fed you with milk, and not with meat: for hitherto ye were not able to bear it, neither yet now are ye able.3 For ye are yet carnal: for whereas there is among you envying, and strife, and divisions, are ye not carnal, and walk as men?
1 Corinthians 3:2-3

When Paul initially instructed the Corinthians, he had only fed them with milk because that was what they were able to contain. Milk does not mean mixing some unbelief with truth in order to make the truth more digestible. Milk is communicating the truth in a way commensurate with the maturity of "unto carnal" saints, which Paul referred to as babes. Parables and dark sayings are an example of the milk method of communicating divine secrets. Both Moses and the Lord Jesus used it in their earthly ministries. Paul used it with the Corinthians. This "milk" communication explains why the book of Corinthians has dark sayings that still baffle people till date. The Corinthians forced Paul's hands.

As Paul started to write what we know as 1 Corinthians 3, he pointed out to the spiritual babes in Corinth, "neither yet now are ye able." He meant that the spiritual babies amongst them, which were the overwhelming majority, were not able to receive meat, which is teaching devoid of parables.

The letter to the Corinthians is therefore an important letter for it represents Paul's attempt to give these Corinthians a diet somewhere between milk and meat. I think of the Corinthian letters as the bridge between Acts and the riches of Ephesians.

Given that Paul's letter to the Corinthians is about how to help the Christian grow up spiritually, it is important that we understand the instructions that Paul gave to the Corinthians about spirituals.

Part of Paul's curriculum for developing the saints at Corinth was his phenomenal pneumatology. The Church would understand next to nothing about spirituals, from a New testament perspective, if we remove 1 Corinthians 1, 2, 3, 12, 13 and 14 from the bible. This gives an idea of how pivotal the things that Paul wrote in those six chapters are. It is interesting that the contents of those six chapters were not spoken by Paul to Timothy, Priscilla and Aquila or some mighty Apostle like Apollos. These studies concerning the characteristics and manifestation of the gift of holy spirit were taught to carnal Christians in order that they might grow up spiritually by laying hold of the singular gift that Christ has given in the new creation – the gift of holy spirit.

37 If any man think himself to be a prophet, or spiritual, let him acknowledge
that the things that I write unto you are the commandments of the Lord.38 But
if any man be ignorant, let him be ignorant.39 Wherefore, brethren, covet to

prophesy, and forbid not to speak with tongues.40 Let all things be done decently and in order.
1 Corinthians 14:37 - 40

In order to appreciate the force of Paul's words to the Corinthians, we must appreciate the place that the Epistles hold in relation to the book of Acts.

Navigate Acts via the Epistles

Due to its historical nature, the book of Acts has the singular characteristic that it does not teach any New Testament concept in any clear way. In Acts, we see doctrine in action. The doctrines are in the Epistles. We should navigate Acts via the Epistles – particularly the Epistles of Paul. We use the Epistles to understand the book of Acts. The student of the Word must realise that the teaching is not in Acts, the history is.

The book of Acts is a chronological record of the actions of the saints, after the Lord Jesus had given His free gift of holy spirit to them. More technically, it is the action of the singular gift of spirit as the saints yielded to its various manifestations. We see that it was up to the saints to use the gift of holy spirit for God's glory. Failing to realise that Acts should be navigated via the Epistles, we are spectacularly bamboozled and awed by the experimental records of the book of Acts.

The records of Acts must not trump the Epistles. We use the Epistles to rightly divide whatever we read in the book of Acts. It is tragic that most of our opinions about the manifestation of tongues and utterance are fully formed before we read any of Paul's letters. We should first have gone to Paul's letters to gain understanding. Then, we are ready to see the beauty of the record in the book of Acts. When we attempt to base doctrine on Acts rather than the Epistles, we dig a big, slippery hole from which it is hard to escape.
Luke, who wrote the book of Acts, was a companion of Paul. In the

book of Acts, Luke gives clear evidence that Peter and John had a formidable ministry in ministering the gift of holy spirit to people. The record of Peter's sermon on the day of Pentecost shows that Peter was grounded in scriptures supporting his flow in utterance. Furthermore, Luke showed that the Holy Ghost fell as a result of Peter's preaching in Cornelius' house. The first ten chapters of the book of Acts showcases Peter as the dominant authority on helping others receive the gift of holy ghost by the manifestation of utterance. The only record we have of Paul ministering to in order that they might receive the holy spirit, in the book of Acts, is at Ephesus. Therefore, Peter is the one we would have expected to communicate the syllabus that Paul made to the Corinthians. Yet, as you read through Peter's own Epistle, you do not find him laying the foundational groundwork on how to minister or receive the gift of holy ghost by the manifestation of utterance.

Peter's advancement was so pronounced that even Phillip sent for Peter and John after Phillip had ministered the Word to the whole of Samaria. The reason is that Peter had been taught things, by the Lord, about ministering the holy spirit to others that Phillip did not know (see Acts 1:3). This teaching was given to the wider Church though the writings of Paul.

14 Now when the apostles which were at Jerusalem heard that Samaria had received the word of God, they sent unto them Peter and John: 15 Who, when they were come down, prayed for them, that they might receive the Holy Ghost: 16(For as yet he was fallen upon none of them: only they were baptized in the name of the Lord Jesus.)17 Then laid they their hands on them, and they received the Holy Ghost.

Acts 8: 14 - 17

A careful student of the Word will agree that Acts is not the clearest scripture to use to explain the link between salvation, the gift of holy spirit and utterance.

That the blessing of Abraham might come on the Gentiles through Jesus Christ; that we might receive the promise of the Spirit through faith.

Galatians 3: 14

The blessing of Abraham, which could only come on the Gentiles through Jesus Christ, was the receiving of the promised holy spirit through faith in Christ. Faith in Christ is receiving the spirit on the basis of what Christ has done. The spirit as gift is the promise contained within the Gospel. Salvation is the reception of the spirit as gift which is Eternal Life.

13 In whom ye also trusted, after that ye heard the word of truth, the gospel of your salvation: in whom also after that ye believed, ye were sealed with that holy Spirit of promise
Ephesians 1: 13

After we believed and received the Gospel, we were immediately and permanently sealed with that holy spirit of promise. Through believing the Gospel, we received the holy spirit as seal. Once again, the Epistles teach that the born again one is the one who has received the promised holy spirit.

Paul told the Corinthians that we have received the spirit which is of God (see 1 Corinthians 2: 12).

Luke states that the apostles which were at Jerusalem heard that Samaria had received the Word of God. This means that the Samaritans had become saints before Peter and John arrived in Samaria. The Epistles teach that salvation is being sealed with that holy spirit of promise. So, according to the Epistles, these saints had already received the gift of holy spirit before Peter and John came.

What do we make of the term "then laid they their hands on them, and they received the Holy Ghost"?

Did Peter and John give the saints another holy spirit in addition to what they already had in the New Birth when they had received the Word?

This spirit that was given to the saints through the laying on of hands on the saints at Samaria was not different from the spirit that each of them had already received at the New Birth. It is not a case of one spirit for new birth and another spirit afterwards for utterance. It is the same gift of holy ghost that already indwelt each of those believers when they had previously received the Word that was now coming upon each of them as hands were laid on them.

Therefore, if we approach Acts via the Epistles, what has happened is that the same spirit that already indwelt those saints was now functioning through them. Prior to the laying on of hands, you could say that the saints had the spirit within. Through Peter and John's ministry the spirit had come upon from within the saint. This would be analogous to my reaching into your bag to bring out an item that you had been carrying about in your bag all the while. It wouldn't be correct to say that I have given you the item. In that scenario, I am making you aware of it in an undeniable way by the power of God.

It is quite clear that these saints at Samaria had not acted like the one hundred and twenty had at Pentecost. The one hundred and twenty had seized the initiative on the day of Pentecost in response to Jesus' forty days of teaching about the promise of the holy spirit (see Acts 1:3-8). Those one hundred and twenty all responded in faith to Jesus' teaching by manifesting the gift by beginning to speak in other tongues. The saints at Samaria had not been taught about the gift of holy spirit by the Lord Jesus (or by anyone for that matter). If they had been, they would have acted on that teaching by manifesting the spirit through speaking in other tongues. Although, the Samaritans had received the same holy spirit, they were passive because they were untaught in the things concerning the spirit. They appeared to be waiting for something when they should have taken the initiative of manifesting the gift of holy spirit.

Peter and John wanted these saints at Samaria to act on the fact that they had been baptised in the name of the Lord Jesus. They were trying to get the saints to act on the gift that they had already received.

Interestingly, Phillip had manifested the spirit by speaking in tongues in such a measure that the Church at Jerusalem had taken note (see Acts 6:3). He had also manifested the spirit through the various miracles which he did. Whereas, Phillip was comfortable doing miracles by the spirit of God, he did not feel as adequate when it came to ministering the spirit to the saints.

Phillip's actions in Samaria reflected the prevailing mind-set in the first eight chapters of Acts, which is that while saints could manifest the spirit in power and in much every other way, ministering to others to receive the spirit was a realm of operation reserved for the Apostles of the Lamb only. Although, Phillip and others saw this as the agenda of God for the Apostles, it wasn't God that set the agenda that only Peter and John could lay hands on others so that they might receive the holy ghost.

Peter and John had a noted expertise in ministering the Spirit through the laws of contact and transmission by the laying on of hands. The more they exercised themselves, the better they got. There is no record of the other saints doing the same in the first 8 chapters of Acts. The record is that at that stage in its growth, the Church sends for Peter and John.

The assumption that Peter and John were the ones who could lay hands on others so they might receive the holy ghost was a man-made thing, which accurately reflected the level of understanding of the Church concerning spirituals at that stage of their history. Perhaps Phillip reasoned that he was a deacon whereas Peter and John were established Apostles. In reality, it was a knowledge thing. The miraculous was in manifestation as far as Phillip was willing to go. This is why Paul had to write the book of Corinthians. It was the Lord's way of establishing the Church's pneumatology on the correct foundation of what has been done in Christ.

10 And there was a certain disciple at Damascus, named Ananias; and to him said the Lord in a vision, Ananias. And he said, Behold, I am here, Lord. 17 And Ananias went his way, and entered into the house; and putting his hands on him said, Brother Saul, the Lord, even Jesus, that appeared unto thee in the way as thou camest, hath sent me, that thou mightest receive thy sight, and be filled with the Holy Ghost.

Acts 9: 10,17

Luke helps us see that as knowledge increased in the Church, the Lord

Jesus instructed a disciple like Ananias, who was not even recognised as one of the seven Deacons, to go lay hands on Saul in order that Saul might receive his sight which had been suspended and be filled with the holy spirit! We know Ananias got the job done because the New Testament records what a mighty Apostle of utterance Saul later became. The Lord Jesus did not instruct Ananias to go lay hands on Saul because the Lord had improved or changed. The instruction shows that there was increase in knowledge, which allowed the saints to hear the Lord more clearly.

The Lord Jesus' instruction to Ananias to go lay hands on Saul was not breaking any New Testament protocols. The Lord sent Ananias because He knew that the gift of holy spirit was the status of power in every believer (see Acts 1:8). The saints acts in order to release that power. The Lord had not changed His mind, method or plan for the Church. It was the Church that had been breaking protocol through ignorance, which caused them to be slow in catching on to the extent of the riches of His grace.

Ananias was a saint, who was also a disciple. A disciple is a product of diligent pursuit and practice of doctrine. Ananias did not question whether Saul would be filled with the holy spirit as he laid hands on him. His major concern was whether the Lord was aware of Saul's reputation as a terrorist.

This episode of Ananias laying hands upon Saul shows that the Lord uses saints, whether they are Apostles or not; it's just that the saints are slow in catching on to this. Every member of the body of Christ is infused with an over-supply of power, which equips them to minister to others that which they had freely received of the Lord. Until the wider community of saints awakened to this, the only saints that responded to the Lord were the Apostles. He had not used the Apostles because of their title but because they knew and cooperated with the truth of the promised spirit as the seat of power. As others became ready, He used them too. There is such a thing as a ministry along these lines also. However, the ministry exists because the singular gift of the spirit is divine capacity in all saints. The ministerial level is characterised by more practice, which results in increased quality and quantity of results compared to those saints who do not practice the manifestation of the spirit. Thus, Peter and John started speaking in tongues because they became saints at Pentecost. Then, with time, they became highly developed with practice and with practice the ministry blossomed.

The value of cumulative utterance

2 As they ministered to the Lord, and fasted, the Holy Ghost said, Separate me Barnabas and Saul for the work whereunto I have called them.
Acts 13:2

What we do with the manifestation of the spirit depends upon the level of understanding of those present. If you have a concentration of saints who understand spiritual things come together in fellowship, it affects the quality of utterance given. The same supernatural flow that will heal or edify someone will awaken something more in another. That flow was used to convey the plan of God to launch Paul's apostolic ministry. The actual words would be ministered through a series of utterances as they went about ministering to the Lord as a group. When they compared notes and the cumulative of the utterances was pieced together, a summary of the understanding that they arrived at was, "Separate Paul and Barnabas for the work". Those five who gathered in Antioch understood the place of using cumulative utterance in setting the agenda of the Church.

The manifestation of utterance in this meeting drew Paul and Barnabas' attention to that which the Spirit had been doing in them and preparing them for.

The monumental prophecy spoken out in that meeting was going to change the known world. Given the pivotal nature and content of this utterance, it would not have been as weighty had either Paul or Barnabas delivered that message. Therefore, I believe that the Holy Ghost would have spoken through one of Simeon, Lucius or Manaen who would have ministered this utterance that launched Paul's

apostolic ministry. Additionally, I believe that this utterance came as a prophecy delivered through tongues and interpretation.
When we operate the manifestation of the spirit in an intelligent way, it produces eternal effects in us. Also, other saints with whom we fellowship are stirred and imparted with boldness to take their own places. Through our utterances, they are drawn to the meaning of what the Spirit is doing in them.

This was the standard of ministering by utterance that Paul was calling the Corinthian Church to when he said, "I would not have you ignorant". The lesson here is that based on their level of understanding, they were able to use spiritual manifestation to interpret the will of God.

The Holy Ghost witnesses

The book of Acts shows that what you will do with a spiritual manifestation depends upon your level of understanding. Things get ugly when these spiritual things are not understood.

Consider this episode in Paul's life:

22 And now, behold, I go bound in the spirit unto Jerusalem, not knowing the things that shall befall me there:23 Save that the Holy Ghost witnesseth in every city, saying that bonds and afflictions abide me.
Acts 20:22-23

When Paul said, "I go bound in the spirit", he simply meant that he had a strong inward compulsion to head to Jerusalem.

Although Paul had a very strong impression or knowing to head towards Jerusalem, he admitted that he did not know in detail the things that would befall him there. He could pick up the fact that bonds and afflictions awaited him but he had no detail beyond that. This shows that a strong impression does not translate to great detail. The sense of danger is one level of knowing. This is quite different from the knowing that comes as clear details of the sequence of event about to transpire. Knowing is in degrees.

There were many saints in every city that Paul visited who sensed the same thing that Paul sensed. Paul knew that these saints were not making up what each person was telling him. He acknowledged, "the Holy Ghost witnesseth in every city, saying that bonds and afflictions abide me" (see Acts 20:23).

Notice that the witness of the Holy Ghost that came through others to Paul was given to him by something that each said to Paul. This means that utterance was involved. It is likely that the various people used tongues and interpretation to disclose to him their perceptions of danger everywhere that he went.

4 And finding disciples, we tarried there seven days: who said to Paul through the Spirit, that he should not go up to Jerusalem.
Acts 21:4

The book of Acts is big on disciples. Disciples practice the instructions that they have received through teaching. These disciples at Tyre also ministered to Paul by something that they said to him. They knew about ministering to other saints through utterance. Again, this was likely tongues and interpretation of tongues flowing together.

What do we make of that fact that these disciples "said to Paul through the Spirit, that he should not go up to Jerusalem"?

In the first instance, "Spirit" there does not refer to the Lord Jesus nor did God literally tell Paul "Don't go". "Spirit" refers to the saints. It means that the disciples at Tyre spoke by a manifestation of the spirit and told Paul not go up to Jerusalem.

The saints at Tyre sensed the same spiritual sensations that Paul sensed. Each saint had been instructed in manifesting the spirit. They did not only manifest the spirit through utterance, they passed across their interpretation of these inner sensations. The saints understood that sensation to mean "don't go," therefore, their utterances said so. On the other hand, Paul interpreted the same sensation and came to the opposite conclusion. The reason for this, is that what we refer to as "knowings", are not purely a characteristic of our spirits. "Knowings" build over time. They more accurately refer to the mind's awareness of that which our spirit knows.

Paul's conclusion was different from that of the saints because he understood the impressions of danger differently. The difference in conclusions reached, was a function of their understanding. Paul's understanding did not mysteriously emerge in his life. It had been built by the Word.

We see the scriptural basis for this in what Peter said:

14 But and if ye suffer for righteousness' sake, happy are ye: and be not afraid of their terror, neither be troubled
1 Peter 3:14

A fellow who is full of the Word already knows that there are unreasonable and wicked men who have the political power that they use as the platform for administering persecutions. We are often persecuted for choosing to spread the Gospel, take a stand on the Word and for living right. We simply proceed with God's plan of joy, choose to be happy and refuse to be troubled in the midst of such persecutions. We are not to be afraid of the terror of wicked and unreasonable men. It is likely that Paul's mind was adjusted to these scriptural facts about persecution that comes along the path of the choices we make when spreading the gospel.

All those saints that said by the spirit, "don't go" are not demonic. They are simply judging and understanding things from a different standpoint to the Word. There is no doubting that they likely cared for Paul. Their minds were not renewed to the truths of God's Word. The manifestations are of the spirit but involve the mind. It was not the spirits of these other saints saying, "don't go". Their spirits, just like Paul's spirit, knows Christ and majors on Him and His plan. Therefore, their spirits would compel Paul just like Paul's spirit compelled him. Even if these saints ministered to Paul by tongues and interpretation,

Paul would make allowance for the fact that their interpretation involves their minds. Our spiritual effectiveness is affected by the level to which our minds are renewed to God's Word. Our understanding of the Word shows up in our utterance. As a consequence, the delivery of interpretation of tongues is often coloured with our bias and the level of understanding. The mind plays a stronger role in interpretation of tongues than in speaking in tongues. It was this important fact that Paul was expressing to the Corinthians when he famously said, "the spirits of the prophets are subject to the prophets." He meant that the manifestation of the spirit is up to you.

Acknowledge the instructions given to Corinth

37 If any man think himself to be a prophet, or spiritual, let him acknowledge that the things that I write unto you are the commandments of the Lord.
38 But if any man be ignorant, let him be ignorant. 39 Wherefore, brethren, covet to prophesy, and forbid not to speak with tongues.40 Let all things be done decently and in order.
1 Corinthians 14:37- 40

It does not jive with the teachings of Paul to insist that there are no commands in the New Testament. It is better to say these commandments are a documentation of the new nature in the spirit of the believer. We are to treat the Pauline Epistles and especially his command that each saint is to manifest the spirit, as the commandments of the Lord. Paul said that the spiritually mature are those who acknowledge what God has said to the Church through the Word. Even Pentecostals have not given the attention to these instructions like we should have.

By referring to them as the commandments of the Lord, Paul wants us to know that the things he has written are at least on par with the writings of the Old Testament. Paul's writings are to govern the life of the Church in a way that the writings of Moses cannot.

Some people think that the only books that the early Church considered as scriptures were the books of Genesis through Malachi. Nothing could be further from the truth. While he was alive, Peter acknowledged that the writings of Paul were to be treated as scripture by the Churches.

15 And account that the longsuffering of our Lord is salvation; even as our beloved brother Paul also according to the wisdom given unto him hath written unto you; 16 As also in all his epistles, speaking in them of these things; in which are some things hard to be understood, which they that are unlearned and unstable wrest, as they do also the other scriptures, unto their own destruction.
2 Peter 3: 15 - 16

Peter had read Paul's writings and he considered them to be scripture. He categorised Paul's writings as detailed revelation of the wisdom God had given Paul regarding salvation!

According to Peter, the things that the Apostle Paul said concerning the manifestation of the spirit were under the category of salvation. Thus, the more we understand salvation through faith in Christ, the better our pneumatology. Peter says we are not to take Paul's writings as his opinions but the very mind of the Lord. The Church is to treat Paul's writings on the manifestation of the spirit as the direct commands of the Lord Jesus speaking to His Church from the Father's right hand. Therefore, even when he was alive, the Churches understood that the writings of the apostle Paul were to guide the operations of the Churches. Paul's instructions on the manifestation of the spirit through utterance revealed the mind of the Lord Jesus to the Church eternally.

The things that the book of Acts tells as a story, are explained in great detail on a doctrinal level in Corinthians. Corinthians governs Acts and not the other way around. Except we approach Acts via Corinthians, we will find ourselves scratching our heads concerning the protocols for manifesting the spirit in the local Church.

Paul spoke in one continuous flow of revelation knowledge starting in the first three chapters of Corinthians and then presented the teaching in a detailed format starting from chapter 12 through chapter 14. What he said was founded upon the writings of Isaiah but unlike Isaiah, Paul spoke in plain speech without parables. Isaiah spoke in parables because he was speaking to men who were not born again. On the other hand, Paul had saints in mind; therefore, he used great plainness of speech.

39 Wherefore, brethren, covet to prophesy, and forbid not to speak with tongues.
40 Let all things be done decently and in order.
1 Corinthians 14: 39 - 40

It is a command of the Lord not to forbid to speak in tongues.

It is a command of the Lord Jesus that manifestations of the spirit are to be administered decently and in order. We manifest them in a decent way that is compliant with apostolic order – this means that all manifestation of the spirit is with edification in mind. Although, you don't need to understand the Word in order to have spiritual experiences, you'll soon become an entertainer rather than a minister except you are trained in the Word to use manifestations to edify others. Paul gives this much-needed understanding to us to fine-tune our effectiveness in utterance in 1 Corinthians 12 through 14. Any type of decency or order that forbids people speaking in tongues is not biblical decency but spiritual illiteracy and disobedience, which must be repented of.

30 If any thing be revealed to another that sitteth by, let the first hold his peace.31 For ye may all prophesy one by one, that all may learn, and all may be comforted.32 And the spirits of the prophets are subject to the prophets.
1 Corinthians 14:30 - 32

This "first", who is to hold his peace, refers to the prophet who has been nominated to set the tone of a meeting by taking first place in utterance. This is the first by designation. It is the order agreed in Corinth. The saint referred to as the "first" would be the one to start the flow. This person knows when to hold his peace because he knows that the manifestation is subject to him and he can pause for another to minister also. He is aware that there are other prophets asides himself who also have revelation.

To appreciate what Paul meant by "the spirits of the prophets are subject to the prophets", we must realise that he used that expression to further explain his core idea that "ye may all prophesy one by one, that all may learn, and all may be comforted." In order for all the prophets to prophesy one by one, they'll have to take turns. One prophet shouldn't hug the limelight.

Paul's "prophet" refers to the mature saints who are ministering to the other saints. These prophets retained the ability to hold their peace by stopping the delivery of their prophecies or their sharing of revelation received in order that the next prophet can minister too (see 1 Corinthians 14:30).

If we stay in context, the term "spirits" in "the spirits of the prophets" refers to the various revelations, utterances and prophecies that these prophets are speaking to the saints. Therefore, "the spirits of the prophets are subject to the prophets", means the revelations, utterances and prophecies spoken by the prophets are subject to the prophets. It is the prophets that choose when to hold their peace and when not to. By implication, the spirits spoken by the prophet are subject to the prophet.

The operations of the spirit are subject to the man through whom they are expressed and the manner of expression reveals the maturity and spiritual development of the one manifesting the spirit. God does not determine the effectiveness of spiritual flow, you do.

Our understanding of God's Word shapes the way that we administer spiritual flow in the presence of our audience.

38 But if any man be ignorant, let him be ignorant.
1 Corinthians 14: 38

Paul had told the Corinthian saints, "Concerning spirituals I do not want you to be ignorant", and yet two chapters later, he says, "But if any man be ignorant, let him be ignorant." Paul said that those who are ignorant by an act of their will have a right to do so. They will abide in ignorance, for they have rejected light. There is very little you can do to stop people who want to be ignorant from being ignorant. A fellow who has received the promise of the holy spirit can be ignorant about the manifestation of the spirit through utterance even after reading the Pauline Epistle.

Covet to prophesy

It is also a command of the Lord Jesus that each saint is to covet to prophesy (see 1 Corinthians 14: 39). Based on the tenor of his letters, one could not really be Pauline and not be superbly heavy on tongues, prophecy and the practice, pursuit, understanding and mastery of the manifestation of the spirit.

Prophecy is the same thing as interpreting our own tongues after we have publicly spoken in tongues. Today, the Church refuses to heed Paul's command to prophesy. Many believe that they can speak in tongues but that prophecy is for a select few. In so doing, they exempt themselves from prophesying and disregard the plain commands of scripture for the saint in the Church age.

Peter quoted Joel at Pentecost and Joel's prophecy said that the spirit would be poured on all flesh as a result of which sons and daughters would prophesy (see Acts 2:16-18). A plain reading of Peter's preaching, Joel's prophecy and Paul's instructions would lead us to say that prophecy is the manifestation of the outpoured spirit. Paul is saying in effect, since you have the spirit, you should follow through with prophecy. God would not tell His apostle to command us to do that which He has not already given us the ability to do.

The command to prophesy means that each saint can prophesy with the same ease with which we speak in tongues; and we can do this as often as we desire for it is the same spirit that manifests tongues that manifests prophecy. Whether we prophesy or not is not up to God but up to us. That people do not prophesy as commanded by Paul is down to ignorance, doubt and unbelief or being unpersuadable about the truth that utterance is ours in Christ.

Gifts come from God, while manifestations come from the gift of holy spirit. God's singular gift to us is the holy spirit. Prophecy is not a gift from God, it is one of the manifestation of the gift. The command to prophesy makes perfect sense since every saint has the gift of holy spirit.

10

THE DOOR OF UTTERANCE

2 He said unto them, Have ye received the Holy Ghost since ye believed? And they said unto him, We have not so much as heard whether there be any Holy Ghost. 3 And he said unto them, Unto what then were ye baptized? And they said, Unto John's baptism. 4. Then said Paul, John verily baptized with the baptism of repentance, saying unto the people, that they should believe on him which should come after him, that is, on Christ Jesus. 5 When they heard this, they were baptized in the name of the Lord Jesus. 6. And when Paul had laid his hands upon them, the Holy Ghost came on them; and they spake with tongues, and prophesied.
Acts 19: 2 - 6

In the New Testament, we get practitioners of manifestation of the spirit to improve by supplying scriptural instruction to them. People practice the things of the spirit better after they have been instructed. It is also through clear instruction that we get saints to start out the first time.

Notice that Paul first gave these people clear instructions in order that they might receive the spirit which is of God at the New Birth. He then laid his hands on those new saints so that they might express that spirit that they had just received in the New Birth. So, if while preaching to a sinner, the sinner starts speaking in tongues, it'll be because that person had first received eternal life, the gift of holy spirit and then that new spirit gave the capacity for tongues.

We often ignore this fundamental pattern of ministering the spirit to people only after we have instructed them because of the myth of spontaneous tongues. Some suppose that this is what happened on the day of Pentecost.

Is this so? Does Acts 2 support the idea that no instruction is needed?

Peter acted on the instructions of Jesus

2 And suddenly there came a sound from heaven as of a rushing mighty wind, and it filled all the house where they were sitting. 3 And there appeared unto them cloven tongues like as of fire, and it sat upon each of them. 4 And they were all filled with the Holy Ghost, and began to speak with other tongues, as the Spirit gave them utterance.

Acts 2: 2 - 4

It makes for great preaching to dwell on those words "And suddenly there came a sound from heaven …"

We think that the secret is in the word "suddenly".

To the casual reader, it looks like one hundred and twenty men and women suddenly started speaking in tongues on the day of Pentecost. It appears that one moment they were all minding their business in the temple and the next minute pandemonium broke out as some external force overwhelmed them all. If Acts 2 was all that we had to go by, we can understand why that might appear to support spontaneous tongues.

Let's observe that the people that spoke in tongues on the day of Pentecost were the same people that Luke had earlier affirmed had been taught by the Lord Jesus for 40 days. After his resurrection, Jesus stayed 40 days teaching them (see Acts 1:3). This bunch that had been trained by Jesus then waited ten days after His ascension to heaven before the day of Pentecost arrived. Pentecost means fifty. It was exactly fifty days from Passover to Pentecost. This means that the disciples had pondered for ten days on Jesus' 40-day seminar. In His "seminar", He had personally instructed them to wait in Jerusalem for the promise of holy spirit. Pentecost came about because well-taught men and women acted after ten days of meditation on the instructions they had been given. Therefore, we see that the saints manifested the spirit better after Jesus had given them first-class instructions!

16 But this is that which was spoken by the prophet Joel; 17 And it shall come to pass in the last days, saith God, I will pour out of my Spirit upon all flesh: and your sons and your daughters shall prophesy, and your young men shall see visions, and your old men shall dream dreams: 18 And on my servants and on my handmaidens I will pour out in those days of my Spirit; and they shall prophesy:
Acts 2: 16 – 18

Although, Joel is not the clearest scripture to have used to explain the events of Pentecost, it is the prophecy of Joel that Peter used. Joel knew absolutely nothing about tongues and did not prophesy about it. Therefore, when Peter quoted Joel as the basis for the manifestation of tongues at Pentecost, Peter is acting on additional information to that which is in Joel. I believe that Peter learnt this from what the Lord Jesus had taught Peter before He ascended to heaven (see Acts 1:1 - 9). The Lord Jesus had given Peter such excellent insight that when Peter quoted Joel 2:29, Peter added "and they shall prophesy" though Joel did not say so. Peter had correctly captured the fact that receiving the gift of holy spirit is receiving the power to prophesy.

Since Peter and John came down for the specific reason "that they might receive the Holy Ghost", we readily see that the saints in Samaria did not receive the spirit suddenly (see Acts 8: 15).

Although Philip had received the gift of holy spirit and had spoken in tongues, we have no evidence he practiced ministering the spirit. Phillip was also growing in his understanding of spiritual things. Peter and John used the laying on of hands to help the saints at Samaria to respond to the utterance within their spirits from the Lord. It would be up to those saints upon whom hands had been laid to manifest the spirit in utterance.

In Peter's rebuke of Simon, he said, "Thou hast neither part nor lot in this matter: (see Acts 8: 21). That word translated matter is elsewhere translated utterance. So, the receiving of the holy ghost means saints taking their part and lot in utterance.

3 Withal praying also for us, that God would open unto us a door of utterance, to speak the mystery of Christ, for which I am also in bonds:
4 That I may make it manifest, as I ought to speak.
Colossians 4: 3 - 4

God's reason for opening the door of utterance is so that Paul would be enabled to speak the mystery or religious secrets of Christ. The reason for all utterance is to enrich our revelation of Christ.

When Paul refers to "door" in "the door of utterance", he isn't writing about masonry, doorframes or carpentry. Paul's subject matter is not doors but utterance. He adds the word "door" to amplify the meaning of utterance in the mind of the saint. He uses the "door" to describe an important characteristic of utterance. The imagery that you are to see is that although the door can be opened, will you enter?

The utterance is the door. So, when we see "the door of utterance", we don't look for two things but one.

We can see the operation of this door of utterance as we consider the day of Pentecost:

4 And they were all filled with the Holy Ghost, and began to speak with other tongues, as the Spirit gave them utterance.
Acts 2: 4

The Lord Jesus is the Spirit that gave the saints utterance via the His gift of holy spirit in these saints. Afterwards, each saint received tongues from that utterance and manifested this as other tongues. So, we see that the Lord opens the door of utterance via His gift of spirit, while we receive that open door by the action of speaking in other tongues. We enter through that open door in order that we boldly preach the revelation of Christ.

19 And for me, that utterance may be given unto me, that I may open my mouth boldly, to make known the mystery of the gospel
Ephesians 6: 19

The Lord always supplies utterance to the saint. The prayers of the saints for Paul would supply boldness to Paul so he can act upon that utterance that the Lord already supplied within Paul. Paul would do this by opening his mouth to speak out the utterance. Our prayers for each other do not affect the Lord's supply, rather those prayers affect the saint's awareness of supply.

Utterance is received through the New Birth. It is like a door, for it must first be opened before we can enter in and speak. How often we enter through that door has a lot to do with our level of understanding and the help supplied through prayer – both ours and that of other saints for us.

When saints start voicing the tongues that they received from utterance, we say those saints are abounding in utterance. Peter and John were sent from Jerusalem in order that the saints at Samaria might abound in utterance (see Acts 8:15-17). Therefore, we minister to saints in order that those saints that we have ministered to might abound in the utterance that they have already received.

Abound in this grace also

Paul used this idea of abounding in that already possessed to teach giving to the Corinthians.

7 Therefore, as ye abound in every thing, in faith, and utterance, and knowledge, and in all diligence, and in your love to us, see that ye abound in this grace also.
2 Corinthians 8: 7

Observe that Paul does not ask God to give the saint a new grace. Instead, he brought the knowledge of the grace of Jesus to the attention of the saints. God's grace and peace is not far away in heaven, it is already with us in our spirits. This is true of each saint whether the saint knows it or not. The scriptures show that the grace of God is equally given to all saints for it is given in Christ and no saint has half Christ or more grace than another (see Galatians 6:18; 2 Corinthians 13:14). The grace of God was received by the Corinthians as the New Birth.

Paul wants us to know that it is not enough to know about the grace of God, which has already been made ours in Christ. Once instructed, the saint is to act on that knowledge by putting the grace that he has been taught about to use. Some saints just give themselves more to experimenting the grace than others. It is our responsibility to see to it that we abound in that grace. In order to bring this about in the Corinthians, he sent Titus to them. Titus was going to cause them to abound by delivering to them instruction on who they are, what they have and what their reality is in Christ. As a result of receiving this ministry, they would abound in the grace of giving.

Paul's statement, "see to it that you abound in this grace", means that what we abound in is a measure of our personal practice and pursuit. Paul is saying that the grace of God is in each saint. Now it is up to the saint to make the grace abound. It is not more grace from God but the putting to use of the grace that we already have in Christ. Peter also strongly advocates putting our knowledge to fruitful use (see 2 Peter 1:8).

Paul described how he abounded in the grace of God when he said, "I laboured more abundantly than they all" (see 1 Corinthians 15:10). He exercised himself in the grace that had already been given to him in Christ. Therefore, it is up to the saint whether he abounds in grace or not.

19 Saying, Give me also this power, that on whomsoever I lay hands, he may receive the Holy Ghost. 20 But Peter said unto him, Thy money perish with thee, because thou hast thought that the gift of God may be purchased with money.

21 Thou hast neither part nor lot in this matter: for thy heart is not right in the sight of God.
Acts 8: 19 - 21

When Peter rebuked Simon by saying, "you have no part in this matter", the word for "matter" is the same word that is translated as utterance in "ye are enriched by him, in all utterance" (1 Corinthians 1:5), so the word means utterance, saying or speech. Since Luke records that Simon believed Phillip's message, this means he had the gift of holy spirit (see Acts 8:13). However, Simon was frustrating the grace of God by reasoning like a sinner. The unbelief in Simon's thoughts and his proposal to Peter blocked his access to his part in the matter of utterance. He had shut an open door by receiving unbelief.

The gift that Simon had observed in Peter and John that could not be purchased with money was ministering by the laying on of hands so the saints could receive the spirit into manifestation. Since Peter refers to the ministry of the laying on of hands as a gift, it means that it is given to all saints.

Enriched in all utterance

3 Grace be unto you, and peace, from God our Father, and from the Lord Jesus Christ. 4 I thank my God always on your behalf, for the grace of God which is given you by Jesus Christ; 5 That in every thing ye are enriched by him, in all utterance, and in all knowledge;
1 Corinthians 1: 3 - 5

Grace and peace already belong to all saints from God the Father and the Lord Jesus Christ. Paul shows that utterance is part of the riches of this grace in the saints. All saints are already enriched in all utterance. This enrichment in all utterance is the super abundant supply that is the inheritance of every saint in Christ. However, not everyone knows this. The knowledge of this enrichment awakens us to the fact that the grace of God is God's excessive supply in giving us His gift of holy spirit in Christ Jesus. We have an over-supply of utterance in the grace of God in Christ.

Desire to prophesy

31 But covet earnestly the best gifts: and yet shew I unto you a more excellent way.
1 Corinthians 12: 31

Paul is speaking to sons as sons. Given that sons already have inheritance in Christ, he isn't instructing sons to desire to be given that which is already theirs in Christ. This desire is not in order that the saint might receive but that the saint might give to others by manifesting that which is already in their lives by the New Birth. This is how saints function as stewards of God's grace.

We have been enriched with over-supply of utterance in Christ. As a result, it is our responsibility as saints to put our inheritance of utterance to use, by desiring its manifestation. This desire that Paul advocates is the mind of the saint becoming aware of the rich deposits within the born again human spirit. It is an I-am-a-steward-of-the-grace-of-utterance consciousness.

Our desire to abound in utterance is measured by an increase in our manifestation of psalms, revelation, instructions and teachings by the spirit. We are to covet to prophesy.

Since we are to covet to prophesy, it means that God does not take over our will in order for us to prophesy. We do not prophesy because God "takes control" but because it is normal for the saint to want to prophesy. In the New Testament, your will is actively involved in ministering prophecy. If you are not willing, you will not prophesy.

You will abound in utterance relative to the degree of your desire. Desire triggers the outflow of utterance out of our spirits to bless our world. Desire does not cause God to give us what to say. It causes us to become aware of what is to be said. The fact that desire is a trigger means that the outflow of utterance is not a sovereign move that depends on God's willingness. If the desire is continuous, the flow will be continuous. If utterance is a one-off phenomenon in our lives, it is because we have not seized our spiritual initiative in Christ.

Peter gives us excellent instructions in this regard.

We want to listen to Peter when it comes to the matter of utterance for he was at the fore-front from the very beginning when men received Eternal life. He was also the first Christian to preach boldly after speaking in tongues. On that occasion, he had spoken for about three hours in tongues. Peter knows what he is speaking about.

As every man hath received the gift, even so minister the same one to another, as good stewards of the manifold grace of God
1 Peter 4:10

Peter teaches about "the gift" and not gifts. It is singular. The gift is the power from on high, which is the recreated human spirit we received from the Lord Jesus Christ. So, he was referring to saints when he said "every man hath received". Peter is not writing to tell us to go beg for God to give us something again. The gift isn't far away in heaven awaiting our receipt during large conventions. The gift is permanently ours. All saints are stewards on account of the divine deposit of the gift of the recreated spirit. He is describing that "I-am-a-steward-of-the-grace-of-utterance consciousness". Our stewardship means that the ministration of the gift depends on each saint. There are too many times that we say, "maybe God is not willing today", when that is not the case at all. This stewardship is a duty we each discharge as we minister to one another. It is our solemn responsibility. We shout from the roof tops about our rights and privileges in Christ and rightly so. However, we are to make a bigger deal of the responsibilities that go with those costly rights and privileges.

Although, all saints are stewards of the deposit, not all saints discharge their duty of stewardship well. Most do not know what they have; therefore, they do not place a demand on its manifestation. Peter does not say that all saints are good stewards. The good steward manifests the spirit through utterance. The implication therefore, is that the one who does not abound in utterance, is not a good steward.

We are stewards of the manifold or diverse grace of God. Therefore, we start from over-supply in Christ. Paul's letters to the Corinthians agrees with the tenor of Peter's instruction. Peter and Paul agree as to the diverse abilities that the Father has placed in His precious gift of the recreated spirit.

11If any man speak, let him speak as the oracles of God; if any man minister, let him do it as of the ability which God giveth: that God in all things may be glorified through Jesus Christ, to whom be praise and dominion for ever and ever. Amen.

1 Peter 4:11

Don't let that word "oracles" throw you. The Greek word means utterances. We are to receive from the over-supply of utterance that is present in the spirit of each saint. The grace is the manifestation of the ability that God has given through His gift in us. The grace is that gift that all saints already received. The spirit of man is a steward; it is like a bag, a holding place, a repository of the diverse grace of God.

This manifestation is carried out by speaking, for each of us is to see to it that we speak as the oracles of God. Therefore, the grace is the ability of utterance proceeding from the saint. Peter's point is that since all saints have received the gift, we are to speak as those that have the divine deposit.

When Peter says, "let him do it as of the ability which God giveth", the saints must remember that "let" speaks of permission. It is not the human spirit permit anything. It is the will and mind of the saint yielding to the spirit of the man so that the saint can abound in utterance. He abounds by speaking forth these utterances that the spirit will give to the understanding. When the man speaks forth the utterances, he has spoken as the oracles of God.

The prayers that Paul prayed for Philemon show us how we can become effective in the discharge of our stewardship.

4 I thank my God, making mention of thee always in my prayers, 5 Hearing of thy love and faith, which thou hast toward the Lord Jesus, and toward all saints; 6 That the communication of thy faith may become effectual by the acknowledging of every good thing which is in you in Christ Jesus.
Philemon 1: 4 - 6

The tenor of Paul's prayer for Philemon shows that there is no mysterious document that has earmarked which particular named saint will be a good steward and which saint will be a poor spiritual steward. Philemon, like all other saints, will write those documents with his habits and personal choices. God's part is done. Through His divine deposit, we know that every good thing is within us in Christ.

We become better at discharging our stewardship of the good things as we use God's Word to educate our minds to acknowledge the rich deposits that are already within us. Just as Paul prayed for Philemon in order that Philemon might manifest the rich deposits, we will find out that a life of prayer awakens our sensitivity to His energizings in us. We see ourselves as He sees us and we become more easily convinced that what is true in Christ is also true within us. This is the trigger that causes us to become more effective in the discharge of our stewardship. It is really up to you how spiritually effective you become. The true measure of our effectiveness is built on the foundation of union with Christ.

We are embodiments of Christ.

Again, observe what Paul wrote to the Corinthians concerning stewardship:

26 How is it then, brethren? when ye come together, every one of you hath a psalm, hath a doctrine, hath a tongue, hath a revelation, hath an interpretation. Let all things be done unto edifying.
1 Corinthians 14: 26

Paul's "every one" referred to the saints at Corinth. Since Paul affirms, "every one of you hath a tongue", we should aim to get our services to the point where everyone of the saints gathered gets to speak in tongues at the very beginning of the service. Through speaking in tongues, we would be acknowledging that the door of utterance is already open. We are providing an atmosphere where the saints can enter through that door by speaking, for there is power in cumulative utterance. Once every one has exercised themselves in tongues, we then use the rest of the service to get every saint to act in a way that corresponds to what they had already spoken out in tongues in the beginning of the service.

The door of utterance is open, keep on responding to the open door of utterance by speaking. It is your responsibility to continually abound in utterance.

11

COVET TO PROPHESY

1 Follow after charity, and desire spiritual gifts, but rather that ye may prophesy.
1 Corinthians 14: 1

Paul's letter shows that in the New Testament, the Lord Jesus has given the speaker in tongues much more control of the manifestation of utterance than we admit.

Let's consider what Paul taught the Corinthian Church about tongues.

2 For he that speaketh in an unknown tongue speaketh not unto men, but unto God: for no man understandeth him; howbeit in the spirit he speaketh mysteries.
1 Corinthians 14: 2

Speaking in tongues is spirit-to-spirit communication of religious secrets between God and the recreated human spirit. The communion implies that both God and the spirit of the speaker in tongues understands tongues. When a man speaks in tongues, even his own mind is in the dark concerning tongues. Except the Lord Jesus gives you the revelation or man discloses it, angels and other spirits are in the dark about the things spoken.

The Lord Jesus shows us that satan does not savour the things of God, he savours the things of men (see Matthew 16:23). Therefore, satan is grossly limited in his understanding of God or the things of God, except through men. Whatever keeps men in the dark effectively limits satan also. This is not alarming since satan is an angel who is as organized and as intelligent as the men that yield to him. This fact is key to how God preserved Jesus as a baby during the reign of Herod.

After the wise men had seen Jesus in the house and were on their way back home, God warned them not to inform Herod (see Matthew 2:12). The reason was because Herod was a king with authority on the earth. God imposed the information-blanket as a way of slowing down Herod's use of political might to bring destruction on the earth. The information given by the wise men would have given more accuracy to Herod's venom. Since satan savours the things of man, whatever information gives Herod more organization would give satan the advantage because Herod was yielded to satan. Satan was as disorganized as Herod for the devil is limited to man's ignorance. Therefore, a bamboozled Herod serves as an information-blanket on satan. This was how God limited what satan could do until Jesus grew up and could walk in supernatural protection for Himself.

Paul's statement that no man understandeth the religious secrets communicated between God and the human spirit in tongues is rich with meaning. It is so encompassing in its effect that Paul did not need to make a direct statement about other spirits. The fact that the mind of man is in the dark about the things uttered in tongues implies a lot. Whatever keeps man in the dark effectively limits satan also. This is not alarming since satan is an angel.

Angels hearken to the voice of God's Word. The voice of God's Word is man. Therefore, angels use man to research and interpret the will and plan of God (see Psalm 103:20). It would appear that without man, the level of angelic insight into things pertaining to God and men is grossly limited. Angels and all other classes of spirits gain insight via man's understanding. If man's mind is in the dark concerning the things communicated in tongues, then satan is also in the dark in relation to that which is spoken in tongues. A plain reading of scriptures would have us conclude that since a man talking in tongues is talking to God and "no man understandeth", both satan and angels do not understand tongues.

The KJV rendering, "no man understandeth him", is a misnomer for it makes it look like it is the speaker that is in view. We usually understand the man who is speaking in tongues, it is the sounds coming out as tongues that we don't understand. A humorous man speaking in tongues does not suddenly become a tyrant. It is the humorous man speaking in tongues. Therefore, he retains his personality. The man is speaking religious secrets. It is those sounds coming out of his mouth that are mysterious. The NASB correctly translates this as "for no man understands". In particular, this means that the person speaking in tongues does not understand what he is saying in tongues when he speaks in tongues. Paul is giving iron-clad guarantees that your natural mind, which is the seat of understanding, will not understand what you speak in tongues out of your own mouth or the tongues spoken by any other person for that matter.

Tongues is the only human sound that the mind of those that speak it do not understand what their mouth is saying. This is an unusual characteristic of tongues. It is the same for all who speak in tongues. Tongues cannot be understood with the mind by merely listening to the sounds spoken (see 1 Corinthians 14:2).

There is nothing that says that it is impossible for someone to be present who understands it. In practice, you'll find that when mature saints are gathered together speaking in tongues you don't tend to have any of them understanding the dialect that was spoken by another. In order to understand what has been spoken in tongues, another manifestation of the spirit called interpretation of tongues would come into operation.

Later, in the same chapter, we find Paul saying:

9 So likewise ye, except ye utter by the tongue words easy to be understood, how shall it be known what is spoken? for ye shall speak into the air.
1 Corinthians 14:9

Paul admonishes us to utter by the tongue words easy to be understood so that the hearer can know what we have spoken in tongues. He is strongly advocating the interpretation of tongues. The saint who hears us attempt to minister in tongues would not know what we have spoken in tongues. Yet, he should know. Paul is showing us that the intention of God is that tongues be used as a vehicle for conveying understanding. If understanding doesn't follow tongues in public expression, the saints have not been ministered to. In order for ministry to have happened, something must accompany the tongues to bring understanding to those nearby, so they can be edified.

Since interpretation of tongues serves to bring understanding to man's mind, it is when tongues have been interpreted, that men now know what had been spoken in tongues. At that point the saints no longer see the minister as an illiterate or barbarian.

Tongues in private and in public

19 Yet in the church I had rather speak five words with my understanding, that by my voice I might teach others also, than ten thousand words in an unknown tongue.
1 Corinthians 14:19

The speaker in tongues is to recognise that there is to be a difference between the use of the manifestation of tongues in private and when ministering to others. In reality, all manifestation of tongues is the same; it is the uses that are varied. We are to use our understanding of the difference between the various uses of the manifestation of tongues in the private life and "in the Church", to bring maximum edification to the Church.

His opening words, "Yet in the church I will rather speak", show us that the Word of God has given the speaker in tongues more control than we admit. It is up to the speaker whether he or she goes down one route or the other. God has provided the guidance on how to correctly manifest utterance but He has given the speaker in tongues the freedom to switch from abundance of tongues in the private life to adding abundance of words in understanding to tongues in public. God has not set how much tongues spoken in public is too much tongues. Paul teaches that in his own estimation, "ten thousand words in an unknown tongue" belongs more in the private life. The principle is that in private, the manifestation would be an abundance of tongues, whereas the public ministry of tongues is characterised by fewer manifestation of tongues and much more manifestation of interpretation of tongues.

6 Now, brethren, if I come unto you speaking with tongues, what shall I profit you, except I shall speak to you either by revelation, or by knowledge, or by prophesying, or by doctrine?
1 Corinthians 14: 6

Paul's expression "come speaking in tongues", means that there is someone coming with tongues and there are those that are receiving the one who has come speaking in tongues. Since others are involved, Paul is definitely describing public ministry to the saints. Attempting to minister to saints by speaking in "tongues only" does not profit these other saints except there be prophecy to complete that which the minister had started out to say as tongues. The heart of Paul's command is that speaking in tongues publicly carries with it the responsibility to bring forth profit or edification after the tongues. He is strong on this because the saint has the weapons to use to bring forth edification to the saints and not just to speak in tongues. When Paul refers to prophecy he is speaking of edification.

9 So likewise ye, except ye utter by the tongue words easy to be understood, how shall it be known what is spoken? for ye shall speak into the air.
1 Corinthians 14: 9

The words spoken in tongues are not easy to understand. One would not have ministered to his or her audience if all that person did was speak in tongues to them. Clearly, Paul's emphasis is about public ministry and not the private life of the saint. Ministering to others by speaking "tongues only", would be the same thing as speaking into the air, since the audience that heard tongues would not have understood what had been spoken in tongues. That expression "speaking into the air" means one has failed to minister edification to others. The one who speaks into the air has abandoned the ministry of edification since the audience do not hear or understand tongues. It is impossible to say that we have ministered to others if all that we do is "tongues only". Since Paul equally affirms that we are not to forbid tongues and we know that "tongues alone" is incomplete ministry, we should anticipate that he will teach about tongues coupled with another operation in order to bring forth the full orbit of the ministry of edification. Paul's command is that in public ministry, we only manifest speaking in tongues so as to lead up to giving the understanding of that which was spoken in tongues.

When we edify others, we have prophesied. If we minister tongues only, we have spoken into the air or not edified them. However, if we interpret that which we spoke in tongues the Church receives understanding which edifies them. Therefore, tongues, interpretation and prophecy are closely related. Predominantly, in the New Testament, prophecy is tongues interpreted. This definition of prophecy as the combination of tongues and interpretation is Pauline. It is peculiar to the New Testament. The Lord revealed to Paul how the giving of the gift of holy spirit changes the Church's definition and practice of prophecy. Prophecy becomes the manifestation of the spirit that gives the understanding of that which has been previously spoken in tongues.

Stated in a crude formula, Prophecy = Tongues + Interpretation of tongues.

24 But if all prophesy, and there come in one that believeth not, or one unlearned, he is convinced of all, he is judged of all:
1 Corinthians 14: 24

Paul's "if all prophesy" means that in the New Testament every saint can prophesy. Since all can prophesy, all can properly minister edification. One thousand five hundred years before Paul, Moses had observed that the ability to prophesy was a direct effect of the Lord putting His spirit upon anyone. This was true in spite of the fact that in the Old Testament the spirit was given with conditions and was temporary in nature (see Numbers 11:29).

Prophecy and tongues are from the same spirit

39 Wherefore, brethren, covet to prophesy, and forbid not to speak with tongues.
1 Corinthians 14: 39

Paul's command to covet to prophesy was not written to a special cadre of people in the Church but to all the brethren in Corinth. This means that it is because we are saints that we can prophesy. All are to covet to prophesy because it is the same spirit that gives tongues that gives prophecy. In the New Testament, the fivefold ministers can prophesy not by virtue of their offices but because they brethren in Christ. If they were not brethren, they couldn't be ministers to start with.

Let's observe some of Paul's instructions to the Corinthians:

I would that ye all spake with tongues, but rather that ye prophesied (see 1 Corinthians 14: 5).

For ye may all prophesy one by one (see 1 Corinthians 14: 31).

Wherefore, brethren, covet to prophesy (see 1 Corinthians 14: 39).

Traditionally, what we emphasize from this chapter is tongues. In reality, if we'll let the texts speak to us, we find that Paul's overriding instruction to the saints is edification, which is prophecy. In public ministry, prophesying is the emphasis of the New Testament. Therefore, we should teach that all saints should prophesy from this chapter and not just that all should speak in tongues. We must not forbid tongues because tongues is how we prioritize and emphasize prophecy.

27 If any man speak in an unknown tongue, let it be by two, or at the most by three, and that by course; and let one interpret. 28 But if there be no interpreter, let him keep silence in the church; and let him speak to himself, and to God.
1 Corinthians 14: 27 - 28

This passage is worthy of our meditation.

We know that the setting is public ministry because Paul said, "let him keep silence in the church." So, the saint in question really wanted to minister to the Church. In this scenario, this fellow who wants to minister to the Church examines himself and realizes that all that he has is tongues. Rather than speak "tongues only" and be described as one speaking into the air, Paul instructs that such a minister should keep quiet in the Church. He is quiet in the Church but not voiceless. His audience no longer includes the Church. He still continues to speak but only to himself and God alone in tongues. This dear saint has effectively taken what should have edified the whole Church through public ministry and turned it to his or her own private edification. That is not walking in love.

Although, it is true that I can edify myself by speaking with "tongues only", I cannot minister edification to another by speaking in tongues only.

While, it is scriptural to "keep silence in the church" and speak to oneself and to God in such situations when there is no interpreter, we realize that this is the second command that Paul is giving this person. Paul's first clear command was for this saint, who is now silent in the Church, to desire to prophesy. This means that in public ministry, the saint who spoke in tongues has a divine permission to interpret that tongue, which is what it means to prophesy. Not all saints will receive interpretation from utterance; therefore, Paul permits the saint that should have prioritized prophecy to speak to himself and to God.

Speaking to yourself and to God is not prophecy; that is tongues. Given that prophecy means to add interpretation of tongues to tongues, the implication is that this person is not prophesying because he or she has failed to see that they are in possession of the gift of holy spirit, the new nature, which is all the weaponry for delivering edification to others. They have withdrawn from interpretation of tongues. They have become comfortable with "tongues only". Viewed in its proper sense, instructing a minister to "speak to himself and to God" means that he is edifying himself instead of edifying the saints! This is a massive step down from the ideal of ministering edification as prophecy. This saint should definitely not despise tongues but he should have pressed into prophesying. This shows that whether a saint ministers in prophecy or not depends on if that minister has been taught to prioritize prophecy or not.

The speaker in tongues who had to keep quiet because he judged that there is no interpreter has stopped short of ministering to others. He had ministry that he could not bring to completion. This person, when properly instructed and helped to see that the saint is to desire to prophesy, would proceed from tongues only to tongues followed by interpretation; thus, not shying away from opportunity to edify the saints.

Rather than attempt to minister "tongues only" and be classified as one who has spoken into the air, the person who is given to tongues only is to keep praying in tongues until he or she interprets (see 1 Corinthians 14:13).

The practice of the saints

Let's observe more closely what happened in the house of Cornelius. Since this is the first mention of tongues among Gentiles, it is worthy of our study.

45 And they of the circumcision which believed were astonished, as many as came with Peter, because that on the Gentiles also was poured out the gift of the Holy Ghost. 46 For they heard them speak with tongues, and magnify God. Then answered Peter,
Acts 10: 45 - 46

The Greek says that they heard them speak with tongues even magnifying God. They magnified God but started it in tongues. The "magnifying" completes the tongues. Peter and his ministerial team initially heard Cornelius and his household speak with tongues and then they heard them magnify God. Peter and company understood that Cornelius was magnify God because they now understood that was what Cornelius and his family had been saying in tongues. Ordinarily, people do not understand what is spoken in tongues (see 1 Corinthians 14:2). Since Peter and his company could tell that tongues was followed by "magnifying God", we can safely say that what was in operation in Cornelius' household was tongues plus interpretation of tongues. Since the interpretation of tongues gives the meaning of what had been spoken in tongues and the interpretation could be summarized as "they magnified God", this means that what they had spoken out in tongues originally was praise and thanksgiving. The interpretation allowed Peter and company to say "Amen" as Cornelius and his family gave thanks (see 1 Corinthians 14:17). Much of our manifestation of tongues is worship and communion with God. If these were interpreted, the interpretation should be worship directed to God but made understandable to the saints who are gathered.

The pattern in the book of Acts is that the public example of utterance tends to show the saints always doing at least two things and not one. In Acts 10, they spoke in tongues and magnified God. Speaking in tongues and magnifying God is exactly the same thing as prophecy. The practice in Cornelius' house follows the pattern taught by Paul.

The Epistles of Paul concretizes the truth of what happened in the book of Acts so that our minds can see it clearly and understand it in Christ.

18 And be not drunk with wine, wherein is excess; but be filled with the Spirit; 19 Speaking to yourselves in psalms and hymns and spiritual songs, singing and making melody in your heart to the Lord; 20 Giving thanks always for all things unto God and the Father in the name of our Lord Jesus Christ
Ephesians 5: 18 - 20

When the saints were said to be magnifying God or to be "filled with the spirit speaking", it means that the tongues that was initially spoken by them became psalms, hymns and spiritual songs, which the saints ministered to the Lord. Thus, the happenings of the day of Pentecost fit in with Paul's admonition to sing and make melody to the Lord.

6 And when Paul had laid his hands upon them, the Holy Ghost came on them;

and they spake with tongues, and prophesied. 7 And all the men were about twelve.
Acts 19: 6 - 7

Concerning the term "they spake with tongues, and prophesied", the Greek makes the prophesying an extension of the tongues. The prophesying completes the tongues.

This is a public setting where twelve men spoke in tongues and used the interpretation of the tongues to edify others by exhorting and comforting them. Thus, it is prophecy.

Let's observe how tongues was expressed for the first time ever:

4 And they were all filled with the Holy Ghost, and began to speak with other tongues, as the Spirit gave them utterance.
Acts 2: 4

6 Now when this was noised abroad, the multitude came together, and were confounded, because that every man heard them speak in his own language.
Acts 2: 6

8 And how hear we every man in our own tongue, wherein we were born?
Acts 2: 8

11 Cretes and Arabians, we do hear them speak in our tongues the wonderful works of God. Acts 2: 11

After the disciples had spoken in tongues publicly, the crowd said, "We hear them in our own languages speak the wonderful works of God." The crowd did not say, "We heard a voice from heaven in our own languages speak the wonderful works of God." The Jews are not shy about admitting that they heard a voice from heaven.

They said, "We heard them".

Therefore, the same saints that had spoken in tongues were the same that later spoke the wonderful works of God. Since, ordinarily, no one understands tongues, we conclude that interpretation of tongues must have occurred after the saints had spoken in tongues in order for the crowd to hear the wonderful works of God. This clarifies that just as in Cornelius' house and at Ephesus, at least two things also happened when men publicly spoke in tongues at Pentecost. The saints that spoke in tongues also spoke of the wonderful works of God. This is also prophecy.

Therefore, we conclude that in public ministry, it is to be expected that all saints who speak in tongues are able to follow it up with the interpretation. The interpretation can be the declaration of God's wonderful works, which would be praise. This corresponds to "I will sing with the spirit, and I will sing with the understanding also" (see 1 Corinthians 14: 15).

In order to properly grasp what Peter is doing on the day of Pentecost, we observe Peter through the writings of Paul. Peter's practice is explained by Paul's writings. Although, utterance is experimental, we cannot increase our effectiveness in utterance, unless we stop being ignorant about spirituals. Thus, in Acts 2, we are to realise that the big event was the sitting of Christ at God's right hand, which became the basis for the giving of the spirit in the New Birth. This gift of holy spirit is the singular explanation for tongues, interpretation and the other manifestations of the spirit.

The insights from Paul's writings and the example in Acts would lead us to conclude that we have "tongues only", which is utterance in private and "tongues with interpretation", which is utterance in public. It is the same born again human spirit that gives "tongues only" that also gives "tongues with interpretation". Speaking in tongues does not come from one spirit and interpretation of tongues from a separate spirit.

In Cornelius' house, at Ephesus and at Pentecost, all the saints were involved with speaking in tongues and the tongues did not occur alone in public. Why then does it look like for the vast majority of the saints who speak in tongues today, all that they have is tongues only and only a select few have the manifestation of tongues plus interpretation?

We want to be biblical in our practice even as it regards utterance.

15 What is it then? I will pray with the spirit, and I will pray with the understanding also: I will sing with the spirit, and I will sing with the understanding also.
1 Corinthians 14: 15

Although it is the human spirit that speaks in tongues, it is the will of the speaker that permits the act of speaking in tongues. Not only that, the mind of the saint can be successfully biased against tongues. In that scenario, the will resists tongues because the heart is set against it. Such a saint is unlearned.

Once we teach saints about the normative nature of tongues, those saints who were constrained by ignorance, no longer resist tongues but begin to flow in its manifestation. However, those saints who have been indoctrinated against tongues never tend to speak in tongues, though their spirits are born again and they are bona fide sons of God. The born again human spirit is enriched in all utterance according to the grace of God but the mind of the one that doesn't speak in tongues has enough wrong doctrine to use to resist the outflow of tongues from the spirit. The reasons are varied but the outcome is the same – the mind is given the ammunition with which to hinder the spirit; therefore, no speaking in tongues.

When the saint is taught the Pauline Epistles properly, the mind is renewed and the will of the saint becomes more yielded to the spirit so that the will no longer resists the utterance that the spirit had always given but had remained largely ignored.

However, many of the same saints that speak in tongues proficiently, do not let the scriptures form their opinion concerning the interpretation of tongues. Their mind considers the interpretation of tongues to be a dimension that exists only for a select few. As a result of this thought pattern, their minds unconsciously resists the flow of interpretation from their spirits. These precious saints are unaware that they are quenching the spirit with respect to interpretation which results in prophecy (see 1 Thessalonians 5:19). The mind and will can be submitted to the written Word concerning speaking in tongues, while staunchly quenching the spirit regarding interpretation of tongues. Such people are convinced that it is up to God whether they will ever interpret tongues or not, just like they were once convinced it was up to God if they would ever speak in tongues. Majority of the saints that speak in tongues fall into this category; therefore, in the majority, there is no speaking forth of interpretation. Their spirits did not lose the ability. It's just that their minds have dampened the fire of their spirits.

It is the same spirit that gives the sounds called tongues that gives to the human mind the meaning of those things that have been spoken out in tongues. The born again human spirit does not only speak in tongues; that same spirit seeks to give to the mind of the speaker in tongues the meaning of that which he or she has spoken in tongues publicly. The spirit of the born-again man gives because it is born of God and it bears the imprint of Christ. The same grace that caused our Lord to give His life for us, causes the human spirit to be a giver like God. Therefore, it should not amaze you that the new spirit, the power from on high, gives both tongues and interpretation.

The saint is to know that interpretation is as normal as speaking in tongues. This means that scarcity of teaching in this area coupled with ignorance is what leads to "tongues only", instead of tongues followed by interpretation.

Desire to prophesy

1 Follow after charity, and desire spiritual gifts, but rather that ye may prophesy.
1 Corinthians 14: 1

In our private lives, there is nothing wrong with speaking in tongues only. However, when ministering in public, attempting to minister by "tongues only" amounts to speaking into the air. Rather than speak into the air, we are to desire to prophesy by following our tongues with interpretation. This is the norm. We are desiring the manifestation of what is given to us in God's gift of holy spirit.

This can only mean that when the saint starts to speak in tongues, the tongues come with interpretation. However, if the desire of the speaker in tongues is for tongues only, then only tongues will come into expression. The will quenches the spirit and no interpretation comes forth. However, if the desire for prophesying was present, then the speaker in tongues can administer the edification, which is the profit hidden within tongues. This edification will be ministered as tongues followed by interpretation. Thus, the speaker in tongues may prophesy. Paul would not have commanded you to desire to prophesy, if prophecy is not already available to all saints. In the light of that you would not need to have to wait for another to interpret your tongue.

13 Wherefore let him that speaketh in an unknown tongue pray that he may interpret.
1 Corinthians 14: 13

We learn from the letter to Corinth that in order to arrive at prophecy you must not forbid tongues. It would appear that the normal means of arriving at prophesy is by not stopping yourself from the flow of tongues. Moreover, you cannot interpret unless you have spoken things that require interpretation in public.

Those saints that do not forbid themselves from speaking in tongues will end up praying in tongues extensively enough so that they start manifesting interpretation of tongues. You arrive at prophesying via tongues. There is nothing magical about that.

Since in public ministry speaking in "tongues only" is speaking into the air, if all that the saint has is tongues, then the saint has been endowed with a supernatural handicap.

If we examine the first example in Acts we see Peter saying, "these are not drunken, as ye suppose, seeing it is but the third hour of the day". This suggests that the first time men spoke in tongues, they spoke three straight hours. Thus, tongues was designed to be spoken extensively. We must learn the importance of extensive and voluminous tongues. Afterwards, they spoke the wonderful works of God in the hearing of the people, which means that they flowed in the interpretation of tongues. During those three hours of speaking in tongues, they were broadcasting thoughts for tongues are sounds that communicate thoughts. The interpretation of tongues is essentially re-stating the previously spoken thoughts in an intelligent language. We are conveying the meaning of the thoughts that we have been speaking in tongues. You cannot interpret thoughts that you have not communicated.

The benefit of tongues is measured by edification conveyed. We embolden ourselves to exercise our ability to edify others through interpretation of tongues by speaking in tongues extensively. Thus, the biggest barrier to interpreting tongues is how extensively you have spoken in tongues to start with. We speak in tongues extensively in the private use of tongues with little or no need for interpretation. In public, we do fewer words in tongues, since the aim of public ministry is not to bamboozle the mind but to convey edification in the clearest of languages to the saints.

Observe that Paul does not tell the speaker in tongues to wait for someone else to do the interpretation. He instructs that it is the person who spoke the tongue that should do the interpretation of his or her own tongue. Although, all saints have same capacity for tongues and interpretation, the biggest difference in its manifestation is the quality of instruction saints have received. Equally as important is the example you have seen in others around you. Most saints are not properly instructed about the ministry of the spirit and the stewardship of utterance. The saint who speaks in tongues should understand that by the very act of speaking in tongues he or she has all those other things that are of the spirit already. Tongues is evidence to the speaker that he is a possessor of the riches of utterance in Christ.

When we minister in tongues and fail to interpret our tongues, we are speaking to the air. Instead, Paul says that it is the person who speaks in tongues that should interpret his or her own tongues. He says "I will pray with the spirit" and "I will pray in understanding" (see 1 Corinthians 14:5, 13, 15).

Do we tell people to shut up if they attempt to minister by tongues only?

Paul did not tell us to institute a tongues-police. We know this is the case because he said that we must not forbid to speak in tongues (see 1 Corinthians 14:39). Rather than stopping people from ministering "tongues only", we should encourage the one who has "ministered" in tongues to desire to prophesy. This way he moves from the room of "tongues only" to occupy the room of prophecy.

What is really going on when one saint gives a message in tongues and another saint steps forward and interprets what the first person said in tongues?

We are mostly acting out what we have been taught and most importantly what we have seen others do. This is worthy of our consideration especially since we do not have any scriptural examples that support this practice. Since Paul also commanded that all who speak in tongues are to desire to prophesy, it would indicate that the pattern of one saint interpreting another's tongues means that the one who only spoke in tongues has not availed himself or herself of the resources of utterance that is available to each saint. Some would advocate that since all who interpret tongues are also speakers in tongues, the one who we perceive to have spoken out the interpretation of tongues has not interpreted the tongues of another person. Rather, they are likely speaking out the interpretation of tongues that they had spoken much earlier. There is also the possibility that they have yielded directly to the spirit of prophecy. This would mean that the interpreter has not interpreted the tongues of another; instead, he or she has interpreted the plan of God for the meeting.

Others, who hold to a more traditional position, would say that one saint has actually interpreted the tongues of another by giving forth the meaning of what the first person had said.

The evidence of scripture is more in favour of the speaker in tongues interpreting their own tongues. We are not given a direct example of one person interpreting the tongues of another saint.

What if the speaker in tongues does not desire to prophesy?
If the speaker in tongues does not desire to prophesy, we are faced with the conditions that prevailed in Corinth. Interestingly, this is the dominant slant that prevails among Pentecostals today. We are not to seek new solutions to this issue. We follow Paul's example and respond to this by not leaving people ignorant; rather, we teach them about Christ's ability released through the spirit man. Until people are taught and given evidence from God's Word, they will continue to follow the pattern that they have observed in others. We should not be afraid to yield to interpretation since the New Birth is the power to interpret our own tongues. We must be bold to exercise our inheritance of utterance in Christ.

27 If any man speak in an unknown tongue, let it be by two, or at the most by three, and that by course; and let one interpret.
1 Corinthians 14: 27

Paul commanded "let one interpret". This can be read as "Let the same person interpret". Some take this to mean that anyone can interpret and whoever that person is, he should interpret all the utterances in tongues. Some others read this to mean it is one person only that should interpret and that is the same person that just gave the message in tongues. The general slant of the chapter favours the idea that it is the same person that spoke in tongues that should interpret.

In whatever way we interpret this passage, in order to maintain Paul's consistent message to the Corinthians, this reference to "two or three" cannot be applied to authorize two or three people to give messages in tongues without interpretation.

In the absence of clear, scriptural teaching, the trinity of ignorance, tradition and fear causes us to quench the spirit and hold back from yielding to interpretation of tongues the same way that we yielded to tongues. We are to teach saints to continually yield to the same spirit that brought forth tongues initially. It is not one spirit for tongues and another spirit for the other expressions of the spirit. It is the same spirit. The great duty of the saint is to bring forth the other things of the spirit by removing the mental blocks that would have resulted in saints quenching the spirit.

5 I would that ye all spake with tongues, but rather that ye prophesied: for greater is he that prophesieth than he that speaketh with tongues, except he interpret, that the church may receive edifying.
1 Corinthians 14: 5

Paul's "greater is he that prophesieth than he that speaketh with tongues" is not teaching that some saints are greater than others. The greatness is already available within the spirit of all saints but veiled in those who prioritise ministering by "tongues only". Those who have done a good job with administering utterance are those ones who do not stop at tongues. Rather than quench the spirit, they press further into interpretation.

OTHER BOOKS BY AUTHOR

All books available on Amazon

Contact Author
sekou@sekou.me